MW00659021

'when Ye Pray'

"WHEN YE PRAY;"

OR,

Lessons on Prayer.

BY

C. H. WALLER, M.A.

M'NEILE BIBLICAL PROFESSOR IN THE LONDON COLLEGE OF DIVINITY,
ST. JOHN'S HALL, HIGHBURY;
EXAMINING CHAPLAIN TO THE LORD BISHOP OF LIVERPOOL.

"The hour cometh, and now is, when the true worshippers shall worship the Father in spirit and in truth: for the Father SEEKETH such to worship Him." —*St. John* iv. 23.

"Lord, teach us to pray."—*St. Luke* xi. 1.

LONDON:
JOHN F. SHAW AND CO.
48 PATERNOSTER ROW.

By the same Author.

THE NAMES ON THE GATES OF PEARL,
AND OTHER STUDIES.
Second Edition, Enlarged, price 3s.

THE SILVER SOCKETS AND OTHER SHADOWS OF REDEMPTION.
Crown 8vo, 6s.

ADOPTION AND THE COVENANT.
THOUGHTS ON CONFIRMATION.
16mo, limp, 2s. and 1s.

GREEK TESTAMENT GRAMMAR.
Small 8vo, 2s. 6d.

GREEK TESTAMENT VOCABULARY.
Small 8vo, 2s. 6d.

CONTENTS.

CHAPTER I.

"OUR FATHER WHICH ART IN HEAVEN."

CHAPTER II.

"WHICH ART IN HEAVEN."

CHAPTER III.

"HALLOWED BE THY NAME . . . ON EARTH AS IT IS IN HEAVEN."

CHAPTER IV.

"THY KINGDOM COME . . . ON EARTH AS IT IS IN HEAVEN."

CHAPTER V.

"THY WILL BE DONE ON EARTH, AS IT IS IN HEAVEN."

CHAPTER VI.

"THE THREE FIRST PETITIONS."

CHAPTER VII.

"GIVE US THIS DAY OUR DAILY BREAD."

CHAPTER VIII.

"Forgive us our Debts, as we forgive our Debtors."

CHAPTER IX.

"Lead us not into Temptation."

CHAPTER X.

"Deliver us from Evil."

CHAPTER XI.

"THE DOXOLOGY AS A WHOLE."

CHAPTER XII.

"THINE IS THE KINGDOM."

CHAPTER XIII.

"AND THE POWER."

CHAPTER XIV.

"AND THE GLORY."

CHAPTER XV.

"FOR EVER."

CHAPTER XVI.

"AMEN."

CHAPTER XVII.

"LORD, TEACH US TO PRAY."

APPENDIX.

The Lord's Prayer.

Our Father, Which art in Heaven, { Hallowed be Thy Name, Thy Kingdom come, Thy Will be done } On Earth As it is in Heaven,

Give us this day our daily Bread,

And forgive us our Debts, as we also forgive our Debtors;

And lead us not into Temptation, but deliver us from Evil,

For

Thine is { The Kingdom, and the Power, and the Glory, } For ever.

Amen.

"WHEN YE PRAY."

Our Father, which art in Heaven.

THE Lord's Prayer is given to us in the Gospel for a twofold object. It is not only a form of prayer, but a pattern for all the prayers of Christ's disciples. "*When ye pray, say,* Our Father," is the command given to us in St. Luke xi. 2. "*After this manner* therefore pray ye," in St. Matthew vi. 9. Consider the things which are here asked for; consider of whom they are asked, and in what order, and adopt this method in all your prayers.

The first command is manifestly the easier of the two, and therefore it is very generally obeyed. With very few exceptions, all who profess and call themselves Christians make use of the very words of the Lord's Prayer, both in private devotion and in public worship. Some make it a practice to repeat the words over and over many times, as though this would insure an answer. It is in the use of the Lord's Prayer as a *pattern* for all prayers, that our practice is defective, and if we are to take it as a pattern, we must make it a subject of special study.

The Lord's Prayer falls into two great divisions. First, there are three petitions for the spread of God's glory over the whole earth. These occupy the foremost place in the Divine plan. "Hallowed be Thy name. Thy kingdom come. Thy will be done on earth as it is in heaven." So far we make no direct mention of ourselves. Our Heavenly Father's name, His kingdom and His will, are the subjects of the former half of the prayer.

For these things we ask that they may be on earth what they are in heaven. And how much we ask for, when we pray these petitions, who can tell? Afterwards we are permitted to speak of ourselves. Our daily wants, our daily sins, our own dangers and necessities occupy the remainder of the prayer. But *we* are not allowed to appear in the first three petitions, except as children of *Our* Father, and thus concerned in all that concerns Him.

It is easy to see this distinction in the Lord's Prayer; it is not so easy to follow it, when we pray. We are apt to say far more that resembles the last half than the first half of this pattern prayer. It is to our own loss that we do so, and to the Church's loss besides; and yet perhaps the fault arises very much from want of understanding. "We know not what we should pray for as we ought," when we speak of ourselves and our own infirmities. Much less do we understand how to pray for the spread of God's kingdom and glory over the whole earth. In this matter we may gain much by spending some thought and study upon the Lord's Prayer.

Before examining the several petitions more closely, let us observe some points which belong to the whole. And first, how exceedingly brief it all is! Very few prayers in the Book of Common Prayer are shorter—many are three or four times as long—and the reason is not only to be found in the fact that the Lord's Prayer is a summary. Its seven clauses are not only seven heads of prayer, but seven actual petitions. The very words are for use as well as the plan. And its brevity is not accidental, for in the preceding verses our Lord had been speaking of the length of some men's prayers "When ye pray, use not vain repetitions as the nations do: for they think that they shall be heard for their much speaking. Be not ye therefore like unto them: for your Father knoweth what things ye have need of, before ye ask Him" (St. Matt. vi. 7, 8). Long prayers are not needed to inform Him, for He knows our necessities before we ask; neither are they necessary to persuade Him, for He "giveth to all men liberally, and upbraideth not."

There is therefore more need of meditation before we ask, to know what we should pray for, than of many words when we have found out what we want. Christians are often troubled by the difficulty they find in controlling their thoughts, if they spend any length of time in devotion. But we need not take long to tell our Heavenly Father what we need, especially if we tell Him often. The oftener we ask the less time it is necessary to spend in asking, and the less risk there is of interruption from distracting thoughts. Not that there is never any advantage to be gained by spending a long time in prayer—our Lord and Moses and Samuel spent whole nights in this employment. But may we not believe that they did so to strengthen and refresh their spirits by communion with God? * Communion, or sacred intercourse with God, does not consist in asking for particular blessings so much as in the study and contemplation of holy things.

The study of God's Word is a great help to it. If those who are much troubled by wandering thoughts in prayer, would first take their Bibles, and after one short but earnest petition for the presence of God's Holy Spirit, would fix their minds steadily for a time on some portion of God's Holy Word, meditation of a profitable nature might often arise, and there would be far more material for prayer, and much more outpouring of the heart after this reading and meditation, than there could have been before. And the reason of this is plain. Unless we live very near to God, we find it hard to pass suddenly out of the atmosphere of the world and its cares and vanities into the presence of our Heavenly Father; our hearts are not always in tune for immediate communion with Him. But His word is always ready to speak to us, and we are not necessarily

* In the case of our Lord, there may well have been other reasons for His nights of prayer on the mountains of Israel into which we cannot intrude.

unfit to listen because we are not prepared to speak. "Speak, Lord, for Thy servant heareth," is no bad preparation for Hear, Lord, for Thy servant speaketh. When we begin to listen for His voice, we shall often find the curtains of His pavilion drawing round us, shutting out earthly sights and sounds. And when these curtains are drawn closer, the glory of the Lord will descend and fill the house of God. "WE will come unto Him and make some stay with Him." And thus we shall awaken that sense of rest and solitude which is the secret of His tabernacle, and forms the best preparation for holy worship.

God's tabernacle of old, the place in which "The Lord spake unto Moses face to face as a man speaketh unto his friend," was a tabernacle without windows. The only light in the Holy place came from the seven lamps that burned with pure olive oil in the golden candlestick: and the only light in the inner tabernacle (which was called the holiest of all) came from the glory of God Himself. The tent lighted from within prefigures the heavenly city, which "had no need of the sun, neither of the moon to shine in it, for the glory of God did lighten it, and the Lamb is the light thereof." In the tabernacle in the wilderness, the only entrance to the Holy of Holies was through the vail. And as there was only one way into God's presence then, even so it is now. The way is still "through the vail," through the flesh of Jesus Christ which was "wounded for our transgressions," rent and torn that through it we might come near to God.

But if we can only come to God through Jesus Christ, some may ask how it is that the name of Jesus is not mentioned in the Lord's Prayer? The omission is only apparent, as we shall see. Do not the very first words of the prayer imply that it is offered in His Name? We can only call God "Our Father" through Jesus Christ. Or, as one has said, "Through the Brotherhood of Jesus we rise to the Fatherhood of God." It is only those who look on the Lord Jesus as their Brother,—their "Friend that sticketh closer than a Brother"—who can truly say "Our Father." The very fact that we are able to say "Our Father" implies a knowledge of our proper relation to Jesus Christ, and a knowledge that only through Him can we come into the presence of God without bringing wrath and judgment upon ourselves. Even the heathen world understood something of this. They knew that for sinners to call upon God without having anything to hide their sins, was to call down His anger. It was on this principle that when the pirates on board a heathen vessel cried to their gods in a storm, one who was present told them it would be wiser to keep silence, lest the gods should discover that they were at sea. If therefore a sinful man comes to God and says "Our Father," it implies that there is an atonement, something that stands between him and God's anger, otherwise he could not venture to come. Again, we can see how the words "Our Father" imply that we pray in the name of Jesus, if we consider how little any one used the words before Christ came. He above all others spoke of God as His Father. It was not often that He spoke of Him by any other name. In all His prayers this was the word He used. In the longest that is recorded He speaks of His "Father" six times. No man ever lived on earth before, who was able to go about in the full consciousness of that relationship. In the Garden of Gethsemane during His great agony He still called on His *Father.* When He was upon the Cross still it was "*Father,* forgive them." Once only He called on the name of *God,* and that was at the moment when His Father's face was hidden from Him. Then He cried, "*My God, my God,* why hast Thou forsaken Me?"—but He commended His Spirit to His *Father* before He died.

And as our Saviour was the first who continually called God "Father," so we use that name now by the indwelling of the Spirit of Jesus Christ. It is because of His nature within us that we are able to look up to God and say "Our Father." St. Paul teaches this very clearly when he says, "Ye have received the Spirit of adoption, whereby we cry, Abba, Father" (Rom. viii. 15). And again, "Because *ye are sons,* God hath sent forth the Spirit of His Son into your hearts, crying, Abba, Father" (Gal. iv. 6). There is an essential difference between this name and the other names of God. "Almighty," "Everlasting," "Holy," "Great," "Dreadful"—all these imply attributes of God, they represent our ideas of His power, His unchangeableness, His holiness. But "Father" is quite different. That name implies a relationship to ourselves. None of the others do.

When you call God " Father" you claim to be His child, to have sprung from Him, to have a nature that was His before it was yours, in short to be a son of God; and this is nothing less than to be a "partaker of the Divine nature," which we cannot be, unless we have within us the nature of Jesus Christ. If His Spirit is in us, then we are sons of God. If not, we are only His creatures, and our whole nature is defiled with something which is altogether opposed to Him and did not come to us from Him.

It is impossible, then, to speak to God as "Our Father," unless we have the nature of Jesus Christ, and therefore the Lord's Prayer is a prayer in the name of Jesus. No one has a right to use it who has not the Spirit of Jesus, or who does not at least *wish* for that Spirit, and *desire* to pray in that name.

To the question why the Lord's Prayer is not ended or presented in the Name of Jesus, we may find still further replies. First, if it be our Lord's own prayer, intended for His personal use, and not only for His disciples, He could not pray in His own name, except by an appeal to His relationship. When He said Our Father, He prayed in the name of a Son. That ground is open to His people ever since He spake on Easter Day of Him who is " both My Father and your Father, and My God and your God." Secondly, when we use these words, we speak the language of Him who spoke as never man spoke. Some have tried to show that the Lord's Prayer is a compilation, a mere *cento* of Jewish petitions; and they appeal to Talmudical writers in proof of this. *But they forget that the Talmudical writers are more modern than the New Testament.* The truth is, that no one can use the prayer without having learned it directly or indirectly from its Author. To pray in the words of Jesus is to pray in the Name of Jesus. Our Father knows and will acknowledge the words of His dear Son. Thirdly, the last petition, "*Deliver* us from evil," recalls the Name of the *Deliverer.* It is identical with the "Redeemer who shall come from Zion," the "near kinsman" of the Old Testament, our Brother and the Redeemer of our blood.

Which art in Heaven.

IN our thoughts about the meaning of this sentence in the Lord's Prayer, we shall find it well to keep in mind His own saying, that "No man hath ascended up to heaven, save He that came down from heaven, even the Son of Man which is in heaven." He can tell us of heavenly things. No one else can. What, then, was His thought, and what did He mean by this mention of heaven in His own prayer?

The words may have more than one meaning. The first idea they convey to us is that of *a certain place*. "Our Father, which art in heaven," *but not here.* Yet is He not here? "Do not I fill heaven and earth, saith the Lord?" and is it not the first thing needful for true prayer that we should realise the near presence of Him to whom we pray? otherwise we shall seem to be "speaking into the air." But a very little thought, and a single passage from the Gospel, will suffice to show that there is another idea besides that of a certain place, in the mention of our Father which is *in heaven.* "If ye, *being evil,* know how to give good gifts unto your children, how much more shall your Father *which is in heaven* give good things to them that ask Him?" (St. Matt. vii. 11). In St. Luke, He says "your heavenly Father" (xi. 13). There is the same contrast with "evil" men in both passages.* But surely it is not the mere fact that our Father is "in heaven" that makes Him better than any Father upon earth. There is a *character* as well as a *place* indicated by the word heavenly. Heaven is a different sphere of action from earth. One of the earliest and best known types of heaven, the Promised Land, may serve to illustrate the difference. "Ye shall not do after all the things that we do here this day, every man whatsoever is right in his own eyes. For ye are *not yet come unto the rest* and to the inheritance, which the Lord your God giveth you. But when ye go over Jordan, then" ——. The contrast between the "fathers of our flesh, who chasten their children for a few days here, after their own pleasure," or as we should say, in familiar language, "according to their light," and the Father of Spirits, all whose chastening is "for our profit," and tends to make us "partakers of His holiness,"—is of the same kind. Thus we learn that heaven is not only a different sphere from earth, but a sphere of different action, a region where things are not done in the same way as they are done here.

No one upon earth can ever have known this better than our Lord. No one can have been more

* The words of the Litany, "O God the Father, of heaven," are intended as a reminder of the same thing.

conscious of the difference between earth and heaven than He was. And from His perfect knowledge of things above, we may say that no one was less likely to feel the need of something to draw Him heavenward while He was upon earth. "*Our* soul cleaveth to the dust." We need everything that we can lay hold of to turn our eyes heavenward, and to raise them to Him that dwelleth in the heavens, but it may well seem to us that there was no such deficiency in the mind of our Saviour as there is in ours. Heavenly-mindedness was a part of His very being. His soul was the true eagle, that "mounts up and makes her nest on high;" that "dwelleth and abideth on the rock, upon the crag of the rock, and the strong place." His were the eyes that "behold afar off." Why then should the mind of Christ need to be reminded concerning His Father, that He is in heaven?

It will be seen that we take the Lord's Prayer as not only a pattern to us, but also His very own—the prayer which expressed His desires as man for men, the sum of all His human approaches to His Father and our Father, to His God and our God. In this light, even the prayer for forgiveness will present no difficulty to those who can accept Him as their entire representative and substitute—the Lamb of God that [lifteth up and] "taketh away the sin of the world." We need not refuse to believe that He said "Father, forgive us," if we know that He said "Father, forgive them." Many a time, if He joined in the Psalms and prayers which were the common devotions of His people, He must have added His voice to the confession of sin and the petition for forgiveness. True, it is not so written in the Gospel. But a moment's thought will suffice to convince any one, without seeking proof from early Jewish liturgies, that no Israelite could have lived thirty years in Palestine at the Christian era, and joined in the common worship of God's ancient people, without making many an acknowledgment of sin, and joining in many a prayer for pardon. Thus He paid the things that He never took, and owned the debts that were never His. Is it a mistake to suppose that He, when He took His place as Head of our insolvent manhood, said, "Forgive us our debts as we also forgive our debtors?" With what wonderful depth of meaning could He give utterance to both clauses. Forgive *us*, as WE also forgive. WE, that is Thou, O Father, and I in Thee. US, that is, us men indebted, and *Me* who have now paid all the debt. Thus, surely, as well as in other ways, God "made Him to be sin for us, *who knew no sin*, that we might be made the righteousness of God in Him." Was "guile found in His mouth," if He Himself led the prayers of His disciples in the words of His own prayer?

But to return to the words which are more immediately before us. Our Father, *which art in heaven.* We may be surprised to see, if we have not already noticed, how often this sentence is re-echoed in our Lord's discourses in the Gospel of St. John. We have already cited one passage from the first discourse that this Gospel records—the private conference with Nicodemus (St. John iii. 12, 13). There is another in His conversation with the woman of Samaria, when He speaks of "true worshippers," and says that they must "worship the Father *in spirit* and in truth." To worship in spirit is to worship, not with the ritual of earth, but in the breath of heaven. Spirit is the invisible force which moves things heavenly. Without the Spirit, we cannot really say, "Our Father, which art in heaven." But though our Saviour asserted His own continued heavenly existence, "the Son of man *which is in heaven*," He constantly spoke as One who made a sharp distinction between the two spheres of life in which He lived, His temporal life on earth, and the life above. He raised His thoughts from this world to that, as systematically and as frequently as any poor sinner has need to do, if he is to live the life that is hid with Christ in God. Thus He says concerning all His words and actions (St. John v. 19), "The Son can do nothing of Himself, but what *He seeth the Father do*." "I speak that *which I have seen with My Father* (viii. 38); and not only does He speak repeatedly of His own coming down from heaven, "I came down from heaven not to do Mine own will, but the will of Him that sent Me;" "I am the Living Bread which came down from heaven" (St. John vi. 38, 51), but He also speaks of His return into heaven as a distinct exaltation which would bring Him greater advantages for Divine action, and endow Him with larger powers. "If ye loved Me, ye would rejoice, because I said *I go unto the Father; for My Father is greater than I*" (xiv. 28); "He that believeth on Me, the works that I do, shall he do also; and *greater works than these shall he do; because I go unto My Father*" (xiv. 12). The words concerning the Holy Spirit are familiar, "It is expedient for you that I go away: for if I go not away, the Comforter will not come unto you" (xvi. 7). But it is not only the coming of the Holy Spirit that marks our Saviour's ascension. He seems clearly to intimate that He Himself would do more for us from thence than He did here, although if He had not first come down to us, He would not have "taken hold" of us at all. And that the power exercised from Heaven is greater than that which is exercised on earth is clear, once more, from the words of the prayer in St. John xvii. 11, "And now I am no more in the world, but *these are in the world, and I come to Thee. Holy Father, keep through Thine own name* those whom Thou hast given Me, that they may be one, as We are." Here it is implied that our Father who is in heaven is a greater "Keeper of Israel" than even His own Son could be upon earth.

This last passage presents us with a further contrast, which helps to make the meaning clear. "I am *no more in the world*," but "I come to Thee." "In the world" is one sphere of action, and "in heaven" is another: even the Divine mode of working is not quite the same in the two. The things that are done in heaven control those that are done in earth. But they are not the same things, nor are they done in the same way.*

When, therefore, we pray to *our Father in heaven*, we appeal to that sphere of action which is in its very nature *above* the powers of this world, and not simply supreme *among* them—which can leave them apparently free to work their will, and yet hold its own all the while, protecting our Father's children, and attaining His own ends, even while seeming to let the world have its way.

And this view is entirely consistent with all our Saviour's dealings with the powers of this world. It has often been observed that Jesus Christ is not, strictly speaking, a historical character. The *world* (apart from the church) *has no record of His existence*, except as a criminal executed under Pontius Pilate in the reign of Tiberius Cæsar. His trial under Pilate was the only occasion on which He confronted the powers of the visible world at all. He held no office under the government of Israel. He was tried and condemned as a private person. The Jewish authorities did not even formally recognise Him as a prophet. Neither He, nor His forerunner, John the Baptist, hold any place in the history of Israel. We thus obtain what seems a paradox, that He, whose name has turned the world upside down ever since His departure out of the world, and whose authority is claimed by all the *Christian* kings of the civilised

* The modern scientific discovery that heat is but a mode of motion, and sound can be represented as vibration, may help to illustrate what is said.

world (or what do they mean by Christian?), lived in the world without touching the fabric of its government at all. In the midst of this world, His life and His mode of operation were always heavenly. And His heavenly power necessarily has a greater freedom of operation in that sphere where the princes of this world cannot come. This last truth is also distinctly stated by our Saviour to His adversaries and to His apostles alike. "Ye shall seek Me and shall not find Me, and *where I am thither ye cannot come.*" His meaning is clear to *us*, "I go my way to Him that sent me." But *they* could only say, "Will He kill Himself?" or, "Will He go to the Gentiles?" Their own world and the world outside they could distinguish. But they could not "see the kingdom of God." And even disciples must be told, "Whither I go, ye cannot come." "Whither I go, thou canst not follow Me now, but thou shalt follow Me afterwards." Yet it is said, "Whither I go ye know, and the way ye know." "I am the way, the truth, and the life: no man cometh *unto the Father*, but by Me."

To sum up what has been briefly indicated. We are taught, when we pray, to lift up our souls to our Father, *who is in heaven*, not because He is not here, but because He is in a world that controls all that is done here, and can control it without ever seeming to meddle with it in any way. We do not ask Him to work by earthly modes and influences, but to work as He works in heaven, to keep us through His own Name, and bring us to our Saviour, who passed through the things of this world, while living the life of heaven upon earth. Thus we throw ourselves in spirit into that heavenly life, which lies beyond the reach of earthly care. The forces of this world cannot touch it, and therefore, when we commit ourselves in everything by prayer and supplication to our Heavenly Father, we are sure that the peace of God, which passeth all understanding, will guard our hearts and minds through Christ Jesus. If He kept us as a Father upon earth, it would be possible, and might be needful, to understand the method of His guardianship. But His heavenly keeping "passeth all understanding." The peace which we know not, transcends all that we can think or know. In the "many mansions" or "abodes" of our Father's house, the reason of this peace is understood. In every mansion and "abode" which our Heavenly Father and His Son Jesus Christ make with anyone that loves the Saviour and keeps His word, this peace flows constantly as a river, but is always unfathomable. "*My peace* I give unto you; *not as the world giveth,* give I unto you." "Not as the world giveth," and therefore at present, ineffably and inexplicably, a "peace that passeth all understanding." Even the "mind of Christ" that "we have" does not explain it. But it flows within us and around us, "a river that cannot be passed over." Our Father in heaven is the source of it, and therefore we are bidden to pray to Him. "In peace we make our supplication to thee," and "beseech thee to hear us good Lord."

Hallowed be Thy Name . . . on Earth, as it is in Heaven.

—o—

THE second sentence of the Lord's Prayer, "Hallowed be Thy name," presents us with a beautiful contrast to the first clause. When we say "Our Father," we think of God as regarding us with all the love and care of a parent, a love and care which are most exercised when they are least understood. This name and this relation include the tenderest affections of man. The words that follow, "Hallowed be Thy name," remind us that our Father has all the holiness of a God. His mercy to us is like a Father's pity for his own children, but His character is holiness, spotless and divine. What then did our Lord mean when He taught us to pray to His Father and our Father "Hallowed be Thy name"? Hallowed is only another word for sanctified. To hallow is to make holy. God's name is Holy, therefore we are to pray that it may be made holy. But the name of God is holy from everlasting to everlasting. It cannot be made what it is already. No man can either add to or take away from the holiness of God's name;

our "goodness extendeth not to Him." And "if thou sinnest, what doest thou against Him?" We can neither brighten nor darken the holiness of God. It is eternal, unchangeable and perfect. But though we cannot make God's name holy, we can *treat it as holy*, which is the true meaning of the word.* We may show by our words and actions that we believe this holiness to be a reality, which we reverence and highly exalt. In this way although we cannot raise the character of our God, we may elevate the opinion of man. The master is often judged by the conduct of his servants. If those who pass by see the servants treating their master with the deepest reverence, or if the world in general sees public honour paid to one man, the world's opinion of that man is exalted, and its respect for him is increased.

To be treated with public respect by those who are around, tends to secure the respect of the world. But to be despised and slighted, to be treated with rudeness by those about us, is almost sure to lower our character in the eyes of men. As it is with the name of a man, so with the Name of our Heavenly Father. If that name is always mentioned with awe and reverence by the children of God, if they in all their actions and by all their words show that they consider their Father to be a God of spotless holiness, the men of the world, seeing them, will be more disposed to think of God in the same way. They may

* Those who can compare the word for "justify" in the original language of the New Testament with other words of similar form, will find a further illustration of this way of speaking.

not indeed learn to love Him or try to please Him, but they will hesitate to take His Name in vain, or to treat anything that belongs to Him with too great freedom, with too little fear and reverence. In short, as the children of God behave towards their Father in heaven, so, for the most part, will the world incline to speak and act towards Him. In this way we see how the name of God, though in itself unchangeable, may change the character which it bears amongst men. Men may think lightly of it, "Thou thoughtest wickedly that I am even such an one as thyself." Or they may think highly of it, "Holy and Reverend is His Name." In this sense God's name can be hallowed or sanctified or made to be holy upon earth. When men treat it and think of it as holy, having a sufficient idea what holiness means, it is hallowed upon earth. When they speak of it lightly and think of it less highly than they ought to think, then God's name is not hallowed, but despised and profaned upon earth. His honour in the eyes of men is made little and contemptible.*

It is remarkable that when God speaks to man upon His own reputation amongst us, He speaks less of the hallowing of His name than of the hallowing of Himself. "I will be sanctified (or hallowed) in them that come nigh me." "I will be hallowed among the children of Israel." "Ye believed me not to sanctify me." Our respect to God's name

* The risk arising to religion from those public religious demonstrations which are not attended with reverence for the holy Name is manifest, and ought to be remembered more than it is.

will always be according to our knowledge of Himself. But whereas there are few who know God Himself, there are many who know His name. To most men in the present life God is not much more than a name. Himself they have not seen. And as they mostly walk by sight, they think more of the name which they can hear, than of the Being whom they cannot see, and more of things which they do see, than of any name whatever.

But we are taught to pray that our Father's name may be reverenced as holy even by those who know nothing more of Him than His name. We have therefore to consider what kind of behaviour on the part of God's servants is likely to make that name hallowed. What kind of assistance do we require from our heavenly Father to enable us so to live that His name may be hallowed in the earth by reason of our lives? In many passages in the Old Testament and in one or two in the New Testament it is said that God is sanctified in His people before the world, or that His people sanctify Him in the sight of the world. These passages seem to arrange themselves under two heads.

God is sanctified in His people when they are holy and happy, when they find God's blessing in a life which is stamped with the likeness of God's holiness. Then His holiness is perceived and respected by the world. Another way is when God's wrath and judgment descend on those who ought to be holy and are not; when unholiness is visited before the eyes of men with punishments that are evident marks of the Divine displeasure. We may illustrate the last of these two methods by Isaiah v. 16: "The Lord of Hosts shall be exalted in judgment"—that is, justice, the execution of true judgment between man and man; "And God that is holy shall be hallowed, or sanctified in righteousness"—that is, by the righteous lives and dealings of His people; the righteousness of God's saints, which shall appear after the pride of man has been humbled and the kingdoms of the world subdued.

If Christians are untrue or unjust in their dealings, they profane the name of their God. "What," say the children of this world, "does your religion teach you such practices as that? If that is Christianity, I can do better without it." But what name is really insulted and despised when men sneer at Christianity? It is the name of Christ, the Son of the Father; and through Him the name of the Father Himself. As our Lord said to His disciples, "He that despiseth you despiseth me, and he that despiseth me despiseth Him that sent me."

It is impossible for Christians to make themselves justly contemptible by unworthy actions, without bringing unjust contempt on the name of Christ and of God. "God that is holy shall be sanctified in righteousness;" but He is blasphemed when His people commit iniquity. "The name of God is blasphemed among the Gentiles through you, as it is written," (Rom ii. 24; comp. Isa. lii. 5.) In several passages in the Bible the sanctification of God's name before the world is shown to be closely connected with the *fear* of God before His people. In Isaiah viii. 12, 13, we read, "Say ye not, a confederacy, to all them to whom this people shall say, a confederacy; neither fear ye their fear, nor be afraid. Sanctify the Lord of hosts Himself; and let Him be your fear, and let Him be your dread"—that is, do not fear as the world does, but fear God. Remember that He is holy, and when you are tempted to do anything unholy, do not fear to turn away. Do not think it necessary to borrow worldly weapons, or use worldly instruments of defence, even if the world should threaten and persecute. "Fear not them which kill the body, and after that have no more that they can do, but . . . fear Him, which after He hath killed hath power to cast into hell, yea, I say unto you, Fear Him."

An important difference between the true God and all false gods is, that though other gods have been accounted great, none but the true God has ever been accounted holy. The very notion of holiness as an attribute of God, proves that some true knowledge of God is in the mind of him who has it. We find these two ideas of God opposed in the oaths taken by Laban and Jacob when they parted from each other in Mount Gilead (Gen. xxxi. 53). Laban speaks only of God. Jacob speaks of a *fear*, "the fear of his father Isaac." Compare the dealings of these two men. In Laban we find dishonesty, covetousness, deceit, uncharitableness, and idolatry. In Jacob we find faithful and laborious service. Jacob had, and Laban had not, the fear of God before his eyes. Laban knew God as mighty; Jacob served Him as holy, though with many imperfections in his service.* If God's people do not glorify Him by their worship and service, if they live in a manner unworthy of His name, in bringing discredit upon Him before the eyes of the world, God does not always allow His name to be blasphemed or dishonoured If men refuse to sanctify Him by living in that holiness which is like Him, He has another way of being sanctified, by bringing sudden judgments upon them. Thus it was when Nadab and Abihu offered strange fire before the Lord, in the day on which they and their father Aaron were consecrated to the priest's office. They died there on the spot. And Moses tells us the reason, "I will be sanctified in them that come nigh me." If men blind themselves to God's great attribute of holiness, He must be sanctified by vindicating that character Himself, and letting His hand fall upon those who have dared to speak or act unworthily of Him.

When we pray, "Hallowed by Thy Name," we must not forget that it is the name of "Father." And in speaking of "the Fatherhood of God," we must not forget His holiness. Here the question presents itself, whether we may call Him our Father by creation, or whether we must wait for that privilege until we have apprehended that He is our Father by redemption. Two passages from the Gospels and one from the Epistles seem to balance these truths.

In St. Luke xi. we read, "If ye then, being evil,

* Comp. Ezek. xxxvi. 17–30.

know how to give good gifts unto your children: how much more shall your heavenly Father give the Holy Spirit to them that ask Him?" The right of our children to their parents' bread is a right derived from birth, not from redemption. The words, "to them that ask Him," contain no limitation. Every one that asketh receiveth. In this passage, therefore, our Father in heaven acknowledges every one of us who will acknowledge Him.

But 1 John iii. 1, "Behold what manner of love the Father hath bestowed upon us, that we should be called the sons of God," shows that there is a sonship which is a special privilege, arising from the presence of that Spirit of adoption, for which we all are invited to pray. And the further privileges of prayer are only for those who accept their Father in Heaven as a Holy Father. In our Saviour's last prayer before Gethsemane, He called upon His Father by this title "Holy." But in that prayer, He expressly said, "I pray *not for the world*, but for them whom thou hast given me, *for they are thine.*" "If, then, *ye call Him Father*, who without respect of persons judgeth according to every man's work, pass the time of your sojourning here in fear." As a Creator and Preserver, He is a Father to all His creatures. To those who ask for His Holy Spirit, He is especially a Father. For He gives them the Spirit of adoption, calls them His sons, and makes them partakers of His Holiness.

We must observe that the words "on earth as it is in heaven," belong equally to the three first petitions, though we generally say them as if they formed part of the third only. How far is the respect and reverence for

God's holiness to extend? What measure of regard is enough? When shall we be satisfied that our Father's holiness is sufficiently acknowledged upon earth? We pray that the inhabitants of earth may have the same respect for God's holiness which the inhabitants of heaven feel and show. But how can we know what they think in heaven of His holiness? God is in "heaven, and we upon earth." We know indeed from the songs of angels, Cherubim and Seraphim, "who rest not day or night, crying, Holy, holy, holy," that the holiness of the Lord God Almighty is a most engrossing object of contemplation and adoration in the world where they see God. But this is all that we can tell. We are taught to ask far more than we can at present understand. When we say, "Hallowed be Thy name on earth as it is in heaven," we ask that the Fatherhood of God and His holiness may be equally and universally apprehended. Now they often seem opposed to one another.

His justice is either overlooked, or looked at as though it were separate from His mercy; and His Fatherhood is preached as though it meant universal benevolence, irrespective of the character of His creatures. Therefore, we pray that He may be known as *Holy* while He is a *Father;* that His holiness and His loving-kindness may be seen, not as two attributes, but as one, like rays in the same beam of light. We cannot understand how this can be, but we know from our Lord's prayer that it will be so, and we look forward to the time when God's name of "Our Father" shall be hallowed upon earth as it is in Heaven.

Thy Kingdom come, on Earth as it is in Heaven.

WHAT is the kingdom of God? And what do we pray for, when we say, Thy Kingdom come?

The teaching of the Bible is so full in all that belongs to God's kingdom that it is difficult to give even an outline of what is taught. And yet, little as we understand the meaning of the prayer, there are times when the Christian cannot help praying it earnestly. Even those who know but little of the gospel of the kingdom have desires and aspirations that nothing but that kingdom will ever satisfy. What did *he* know of the kingdom of Christ, who said to Jesus in the hour when He seemed furthest from it, "Lord, remember me when thou comest in Thy kingdom?" To many Christians the prospect of the kingdom is obscured by the fact that they set the final judgment of all mankind between themselves and the coming of that kingdom. And yet how many times do the Psalms and prophets call upon all creation to *rejoice*, because "the Lord reigneth!"

The first mention of the kingdom in Holy Scripture seems to put everything at once in its right place. Man's destiny was God's kingdom. "Let us make man in our image, after our likeness, and *let them have dominion.*" That is the primeval decree for the establishment of the kingdom of God. Man was to be made "in God's image," that he might be *able* to represent his Maker. He was to be trained "after God's likeness," that he might be *fit* to represent him. When that is accomplished, he is to have dominion over the works of God's hands; and He will put all things under his feet. The first man in whom this is accomplished is "*the last Adam,*" and with the last Adam all His children shall reign, as kings and priests unto God and His Father, for ever and ever.

The effect of this dominion will be to stamp the likeness of God on everything, and to conform all creation to His will. When all God's vicegerents are like Him in character, all the universe will be brought into harmony with the counsel of His will. There seems to be a hint of this in the word used for kingdom in the New Testament. Originally the Greek word for kingdom seems traceable to a Hebrew root, which has not only the meaning of ordering and ruling, but also of *making like.* The precise connection of the two ideas is not agreed upon by scholars, but it exists, and presents no difficulty to the believer. All real government is the *assimilation* of those that are ruled to the character of their ruler.

The kingdom of God is His making other things like Himself. When it comes into the world, or into the soul of man, it stamps them with His likeness, with His royal attribute of *holiness.* When God first formed a *nation* for Himself, He promised that if they would obey His voice they should be to Him "a kingdom of priests, and a holy nation" (Ex. xix. 6). "A kingdom of priests," that is, of persons whose office it is to bring Him gifts, and to consecrate all that is brought to them to His use. And "an holy nation." Its character is to bear a mark which no one can imitate, that holiness which is owned alike by angels, men, and devils, to be the very essence of the character of God. It is the one mark which Satan cannot counterfeit. He is often transformed into "an angel of light," but holiness baffles imitation. A holy man is a temple, a habitation, of the holy Spirit of God. Much is foretold by the prophets and in the Psalms concerning the power, and spread, and duration of God's kingdom. And besides this notice of its holiness, all Scripture bears one testimony concerning its moral character. "The sceptre of Thy kingdom is a *right* sceptre" (Psalm xlv. 6). "Behold a King shall reign in righteousness, and princes shall rule in judgment." *Righteousness* is the very beginning of *holiness.* The first step for fallen man to take towards a state of salvation is to step into Christ's righteousness. The one testimony wrung from the witnesses of our Lord's death concerning His character was, that "certainly this was a *righteous* man" (St. Luke xxiii. 47). The one thing that none could find in Him was an offence against the rights of His neighbour. Those who "seek first the kingdom of God," seek "His *righteous-*

ness" (St. Matt. vi. 33). And when St. Paul tells us what that kingdom is, he gives the same testimony, "The Kingdom of God is not meat and drink, but *righteousness*, and peace, and joy, in the Holy Ghost."

It is this which calls forth the rejoicings of the Psalmist at His coming. "He cometh to judge the earth. With righteousness shall He judge the world, and the people with equity."

The coming of this kingdom, when really believed and regarded as the end of our life-training here, gives a meaning to much that is otherwise perplexing, and affords a resting-place to the highest cravings of the human heart. There is far too little meaning, in the expectations that many Christians have, of what they call heaven. "To go to heaven when we die," what is it? One perpetual service of praise and thanksgiving, a reunion of the disciples who were parted by death or the changes of life here; a rest from labour, and companionship with those who, now victorious, have the tale of many a conflict to tell? Or, is it the full revelation of the life and work of our Redeemer, of which we know so little? Is it the society of saints and angels, and of Him who is the King of both? Doubtless all this is before us. But is there nothing said of work for the strong? Rest for the weary ceases to be rest when weariness is over. The love of active life returns. Will there be *nothing to be done* for God in the kingdom of heaven? Surely there will. And one of the first pictures presented to us in that kingdom is a picture of the world of human beings ordered and governed righteously; abuses put down, miseries relieved, oppression driven out and rendered impossible. We look, not only for heaven but for an earth, "wherein dwelleth righteousness." And the kingdom which God has promised to them that love Him is not limited in time or space. It begins here, but where does it end? "Nothing not put under Him," and "we shall reign with Him," are wide sayings, and open a wide prospect. "Know ye not that we shall judge angels?" that "the saints shall judge the world?" "judge," *i.e.*, rule and regulate, not merely sentence to bliss or woe.

We know not how far the forces of creation may be subjected hereafter to human control. "Thou hast put *all* things under His feet"—so the decree runs. And when we consider the manifold and divers occupations, many of them connected with the works of God here, in which men's powers and faculties are trained, it is difficult to think that all this preparation of man's understanding is to be wasted, or to have no bearing on the life to come. It seems more natural to believe that what is learned here is learned for the sake of a life hereafter. Even though the actual knowledge of the human mind, or what is accounted knowledge here, shall be so suspended as to vanish away, the effect of learning to know need not vanish. There are promises to the patriarchs, and to Christ, and to us, which can only be fulfilled by a consummation and perfection of all creation, beginning with the heavens and earth, which God created for man's abode. If the appearing of our Saviour is to be only the *end* of this visible globe, it is difficult to see how a large part of the promises and prophecies of Holy Scripture are ever to be fulfilled.

In this present world, the growth of God's kingdom is the growth of the divine life in the heart of man. There are in Scripture several different figures to describe God's kingdom upon earth. We find it represented by the three kingdoms of Nature, the mineral, the vegetable, and the animal. The Order of life in these figures ascends higher and higher. Beginning with the kingdom of stone, we find the foundation laid, the living stones resting with their whole weight upon it, and thus "growing unto an holy temple in the Lord." Or, we have the vine in the garden of the Lord, and the wild branches grafted in and filled with pleasant fruits, until they become "a fountain of gardens, a well of living waters, and streams from Lebanon." Or, again, we have the Lord Jesus Christ spoken of as the Head of the body—His people as His members, united by one Spirit into one body, to be raised up by His own power to share His glory, when "the kingdoms of this world are become the kingdoms of our Lord and of His Christ."

And in all these representations we see what the LIFE is. It is the holy Spirit of God. *This* it is that seals one stone to another in the living temple. *This* fills the branches with the life of Christ, the true Vine, whose fruits are "fruit of the Spirit." *This* is the very fatness of the true olive-tree. So again it is with the body of Christ. The Holy Spirit is the essence of its union. All the various members have their work assigned to them, and the power to perform it from the Holy Spirit. Thus, beginning with the living stones, we go on to fruitful trees, and come last of all to living men. Then, in the final stage of all, there seems to be revealed in the Word of God something like what we see in Nature, when the life of the age that is past is set fast for ever in the stones of the age yet to be. Only in God's kingdom this can come to pass without death. For what do we see in the book of Revelation in the new heavens and the new earth?

The new Jerusalem descends from God out of heaven, "prepared as a *Bride* adorned for her Husband." And the beauties of that Bride are presented to us in the likeness of every precious jewel that we know, with some, perhaps, that we do not know, and all the most valued productions of the mineral world. The whole effect is like a solid body of light, a "jasper stone, clear as crystal." The brightness is beyond conception. "The city hath no need of the sun nor of the moon to shine in it, for the glory of God doth lighten it." The gates of it are ever open. Through twelve pearly openings the eternal glory is ever streaming, and the kingdom, thus beautiful beyond thought, shines on throughout the ages of ages for ever and ever. Into this form the life that we now live will "*crystallise*" (I use the very word of the original) if we live by faith in the Son of God. It is not death that we look for. In the golden city there is living water, and there are living trees; the tree of life bearing twelve manner of fruits, "yielding her fruit every month, and the leaves of the tree are for the healing of the nations." There is also, still higher, the life of man in all its beauty; for the whole city is "the Bride, the Lamb's Wife." The city is full of inhabitants. It is set in the midst of the "new heavens and the new earth, wherein dwelleth righteousness." "The nations shall walk in the light of it. The kings of the earth," that is those who are Kings and Priests unto God, "do bring their glory and honour into it." Of this fair city we are called to be citizens. The freedom of it belongs to all the children of God. The heavenly Jerusalem is their metropolis. From thence we expect a Saviour, the Lord Jesus Christ, who hath called us to His kingdom and glory, and opened the Kingdom of Heaven to all believers.

The beginning of the kingdom of Christ is presented to us under these different figures in holy Scripture. But all these representations are of things which *begin* on earth, and ascend into the heavenly kingdom. It may be profitable for us to turn our thoughts to the kingdom as it now exists in heaven, the kingdom for which we pray that it may be established upon this earth *as it is in heaven*. Let us then endeavour to realise, as far as we can, what kind of existence the life of our glorified Redeemer may be. The reality is of course far above our very highest thoughts. It hath not entered into the heart of man to conceive the things which God "hath prepared for them that love Him;" much less to conceive what He who is preparing them, Himself enjoys. But the Lord who reigns in glory is one and the same Jesus who was taken up from earth.

The Man of Sorrows and the Lord of glory are not two, but one Christ. And whatever the Son of Man is now He is only that for which His earthly existence prepared Him. "He made Himself of no reputation, and took upon Him the form of a servant, and was made in the likeness of man. And being found in fashion as a man, He humbled Himself, and became obedient unto death, even the death of the Cross. WHEREFORE God also hath highly exalted Him, and given Him a name which is above every name: That in the name of Jesus every knee should bow, of things in heaven, and things in earth, and things under the earth; and that every tongue should confess that Jesus Christ is Lord, to the glory of God the Father" (Phil. ii. 7–11). May we then venture to ask what kind of employments occupy the energies of the glorified Redeemer of mankind? Of some of them we can know nothing. We can only guess at those which concern our salvation, the completion of the work which He began below and is now finishing above. We have before referred to the place which He is preparing for us, and its glories. The hints given us in "the sea of glass," "the golden city," "the tree of life," and "the pure river," cannot be more than hints, of things inconceivable to man, but prepared according to the greatness of our God. "For God is not *ashamed to be called their God: for He hath prepared for them a city*" (Heb. xi. 16). These things are a part of the furniture of the place which He has gone to prepare. But let us remember that every impulse of the Divine Spirit which has been the life of the whole Church of God since the day of Pentecost has come through the Lord Jesus, and has been, so to speak, an act of His will. Every noble thought, every glorious hope, every living word uttered or expressed by Apostles, Evangelists, Martyrs, Saints, came to them through the Son of Man. The true prayers and true teachings of His servants are all the expressions of His mind. And not the words only, but all the noble deeds of faith and love and patience and godliness that have been done by the saints on earth have been part of the employment of the Son of Man that is in heaven. All that the members of Christ have done on earth, has been the doing of their Head in heaven. But not only this, all the light and happiness that the saints of Christ have received either on earth, or in Paradise, they have received from Him. Every thought of comfort in the time of trial, on the bed of sickness, in the prison, in the torment, at the stake, has come to the Saints and Confessors and Martyrs of Jesus Christ directly and consciously from Him. He has thought it before it entered their minds. He has felt its brightness before He made it shine on them. And the happiness of every triumphant deathbed, the glory on the face of every departing Saint, has been a beam from the glory of the Saviour, a ray of triumph from His great Victory. He felt the triumph before it shone in the face of His people. And this suggests another of His employments. Every soul that has passed the waves of this troublesome world since the ascension of our Saviour has been received by *Him* in Paradise. Do they come "to the innumerable company of angels" and the city of the living God? They go to "*Jesus*" also. Every longing Saint that has departed, has gone "to be *with Christ*," to behold "Him and not another!" He has received every member of the great multitude whose robes are washed and made white for the last time, whose last sin is forgiven, whose last victory is won. Recount also the innumerable prayers and special requests that have gone up to the Lord Jesus, and to the Father in the Name of Jesus, from the members of His Church, in the inconceivable number of their wants and anxieties and cares. All these have passed through His hands.

Count up the many struggling souls who have cried to Him in darkness, who have clung to Him in the agony of entering the strait and narrow way. Throughout the progress of every distressing case the Son of Man has had the fullest knowledge, has given the fullest sympathy. The care of all the souls in all the Churches has been upon the Great Shepherd. He has sought every one that was lost, and kept every one that was found. From the moment when they were gathered from the dark mountains till they entered the one flock, not one of the whole number has been out of the Saviour's sight. He knows the works and the ways of all!

And yet this is but a small portion. There are mysteries in His present work of which we can only guess the existence without attempting to fathom what they are. The innumerable company of angels are *sent forth* to minister for them who shall be heirs of salvation. Who is it that *sends* them?

who appoints their several duties and receives the account of their work? If they are sent for the sake of the "heirs of salvation," surely they must be directed by the "Captain of Salvation," surely their various stations and duties must be assigned by Him. Here is a whole department of the government of our Lord Jesus of which we know nothing, except that it is under His charge. And not only the angels but all principalities and powers are subject to His control. What of the evil spirits, the enemies of His Church? Does He take no notice of their movements? Has He no employments respecting them? And then "He is before *all things*, and by Him all things consist." Worlds that we cannot count, besides our own world, are ruled by His authority and upheld by His power. And there is, above all these things, a subject which is unapproachable—His intercourse and communion with the Father, communion of which one glimpse is given us in His last prayer in the 17th chapter of St. John; a glimpse sublime beyond all comparison, but affording no notion of the full extent of that communion now! And in the midst of these manifold occupations, none of them ever broken by need of rest, none ever limited by lack of power, there is the ever-varying, never-ending harmony of the praise of angels, the Holy, Holy, Holy of the Seraphim, the voice of harpers harping, the heavenly music of which the bare description is melody itself. There are the fresh outbursts of rejoicing begun by the Saviour Himself over every sinner that repenteth. There is the gladness of repeated victory as Satan is again and again frustrated by the blood of the Atonement. There is the constant memory of the precious death and passion. There is the perpetual consciousness of propitiating power which must belong to "the Lamb of God."

All these things together, and an infinity besides of which we never dream,—what a view do these afford us of the life of the Son of Man who is the "heir of all things," whose kingdom we desire to come upon earth *as it is in heaven.*

And if we turn from the employments of heaven back to earth, how many things there are which seem to be at a standstill, and in which it seems impossible to advance any further, until the coming of the Kingdom and the King. First of all perhaps in the place which it holds in prophecy, there is the state of God's ancient people whom He chose for His own inheritance, and the place and the country of which He said "My name shall be there." As regards all God's promises to His own people we are waiting until the Lord come. "As it is written, There shall come out of Zion the Deliverer, and shall turn away ungodliness from Jacob." When Christ departed from His country in Galilee and from His temple at Jerusalem, He said, "Behold, your house is left unto you desolate, and verily I say unto you, ye shall not see *Me* until the time come when ye shall say, "Blessed is He that cometh in the name of the Lord." The Jews therefore are waiting, whether consciously or unconsciously, for the coming of their Deliverer. Their affairs are practically at a standstill "till He come."

Turn to the Gentiles. Look at the kingdoms of the earth in which the kingdom of heaven, like the leaven in the three measures of meal, has been working all these years. Why is it that amid all the pressure and the strife of nations, all that is won by war, and all that is established by peace, there is not one single nation in Europe *satisfied* with its present state, nor perhaps one large class of any civilised community contented and at rest. What is it that we all want? We want a righteous government, the due acknowledgment of all rights and claims. Well, and is it not written that "A king shall reign in righteousness, and princes shall rule in judgment?" "Do ye not know that the saints shall judge the world?" "The saints of the Most High shall take the kingdom, and possess the kingdom for ever, even for ever and ever." "The kingdom of the God of heaven shall break in pieces and consume all these kingdoms, and it shall stand for ever." But how, and when? And what is to inaugurate the change? And what do we wait for? We wait for the coming of the Lord Jesus Christ. There is no hope of a final settlement until He come. The heaven must receive Him until that final settlement and re-adjustment of all things, when the kingdoms of this world shall become the kingdoms of our Lord and of His Christ, and He shall reign for ever and ever. We are just waiting, Jews and Gentiles alike, at a standstill, waiting until He come. Turn from Jew and Gentile to the state of the Church of Christ—His visible Church on earth. Is its condition any more settled and consolidated? Are its members any more contented and at rest than the kingdoms of this world? If they are, what mean the unhappy divisions and dissensions and disputations on all sides? They may be signs of vitality perhaps, and better than mere apathy and slumber, but they are not the tokens of satisfaction or repose. "*We* are not come to the *rest* and to the inheritance which the Lord hath promised. *There* we shall not do after all the things that we do here this day, every man whatsoever is right in his own eyes." No, "there *remaineth*"—what is not yet inaugurated—"there remaineth the keeping of a Sabbath for the people of God." We can really *settle* nothing now. Is it not written, "Judge nothing before the time *until the Lord come?*"

Turn from the outward and apparent confusion of the Church on earth to the contemplation of that other portion of it which is perhaps now by far the larger portion, the Church on the other side of the river, in the Paradise of God.

There they certainly "rest from their labours:" and "they are in peace." But are not *they* also waiting and longing for the coming of the Lord? Such of them as suffered for Christ here on earth, and "were tortured," as many have been, "not accepting deliverance, that they might obtain a better resurrection," have they nothing in prospect for which they long, and to which they look forward until the Lord come? What was the meaning of the voice that St. John heard from "the souls under the altar, of them that were slain for the Word of God, and for the testimony which they held?" "How long, O Lord, holy and true, dost Thou not judge and avenge our blood on them that dwell on the earth? And white robes were given unto every one of them; and it was said unto them, that they should rest yet for a little season, until their fellow-servants also and their brethren, that should be killed as they were, should be fulfilled;" that is, "*until He come*" who shall make all these things to cease on earth, even to the ends of the world. The noble army of Martyrs not yet risen, wait in Paradise for their perfect consummation and bliss until the Lord shall come. And those others of the departed who may perhaps have less personal objection to the order of things here,—are *they* satisfied to let things be as they are? What was the topic of absorbing interest with Moses and Elias who appeared in glory on the Mount of Transfiguration with our Lord? To what did they look forward? They "spake of His *exodus* which He should accomplish at Jerusalem." And now that His sufferings are long since over, have they nothing to look for still? Do they speak nothing with Him in Paradise of the glories that shall follow, of the kingdom that is to come? Do the Apostles never look forward to the thrones on which they shall sit "when the Son of Man shall sit on the throne of His glory?" Has Moses forgotten "the recompense of the reward" to which he had respect when he "forsook the treasures of Egypt?" Has St. Paul forgotten "the crown of righteousness which the Lord, the righteous Judge, shall give" him at *that day*, a day which has not yet come? No! the Church militant may forget to think of the meaning of that prayer which the Lord has taught us. The Church triumphant does *not* forget, we may be certain, to pray "Thy kingdom come."

And what are we to say of the individual members of Christ on earth, those who belong not only to the outward and visible body, but who are in spirit one with Him, and therefore already come to the heavenly Jerusalem in heart and mind—"whose conversation is in heaven?" Are *they* satisfied to remain as they are? *No!* If "the whole creation groaneth and travaileth in pain together until now," so also they that "have the first-fruits of the Spirit"—the kingdom of God within them—"they also groan within themselves waiting for their adoption, that is the redemption of their body." And the limit of this groaning is the coming of "our Saviour the Lord Jesus Christ, who shall change the body of our humiliation:" that body which is the sphere of all our trials and perplexities, the occasion of most of our temptations. We look for the coming of the Saviour who shall change it, and make it "like the body of His glory, according to the mighty working whereby He is able even to subdue all things to Himself."

And last of all our Saviour Himself is waiting for that day and hour whereof "no man knoweth, no not the angels in heaven, neither the Son; but the Father." Jehovah hath said unto our Lord, "Sit on My right hand, *until* I make Thine enemies Thy footstool." *He* also waits to see all things put under Him, until the day shall come when once more "His feet shall stand upon the Mount of Olives," so that in the place where He sowed in tears, where once He went on His way weeping, "He may come again with rejoicing and bring His sheaves with Him." It is His desire that these things may be accomplished. It is long since He said, "Father, I will that they also whom Thou hast given Me be with Me where I am." But they cannot all be together until He comes again "to receive them unto Himself, that where He is, there they may be also." Thus then all creation groaneth and travaileth, waiting for Him who longs to draw all unto Himself, and to be received by all. "*We*" also, "according to His promise, look for new heavens and a new earth wherein dwelleth righteousness." "Wherefore, beloved, seeing that we look for such things," let us "be diligent, that we may be found of Him in peace without spot and blameless."

Thy will be done on Earth, as it is in Heaven.

—o—

THERE is no petition in the Lord's Prayer which conveys a more distinct impression to the Christian's mind than this. Even apart from the well-known and beautiful hymn of which it forms the burden, it seems naturally to remind us of some of the darker passages of this transitory life. We associate it with times of bereavement and sorrow, when hearts are sore, idols broken, hopes cut off, loved ones parted. We think of some one who was perhaps disposed to forget God in the bright sunshine of prosperity, suddenly brought to himself in the clouds of adversity, looking helplessly around, but hardly able to look up, and endeavouring with pain and difficulty to spell out the prayer which conscience tells him it is time to learn, "Thy will be done."

Now we have no desire to meddle with ancient land-marks, least of all with those which we know it is impossible to remove. And we cannot say that "Thy will be done" is not an appropriate petition for times like these. When the Lord that "gave," hath also "taken away," and we who have received good, are called upon to "receive evil" at His hands, we have learned by no mean example, that we should "bless the name of the Lord."

Yet it is a very great mistake to suppose that this is the whole and sole meaning of the third petition in the Lord's Prayer. No doubt it does express the resignation of God's children when their heavenly Father has chastised them in His love. But is this all? Let us compare the two former petitions. "Hallowed be Thy name." Because God's name is not hallowed by all persons in all places, we pray that what as yet is not, may come to pass. "Thy kingdom come." The fact that we pray for it shows that we believe it has not yet come. Does not the same rule apply to the third petition? If God's will *is* done already, what is the use of praying that it *may* be done by and by? But if our only idea of God's will is some loss we have suffered, or some disappointment which we consider to be God's will because we are perfectly certain it is not ours, what is the object of praying that His will may be done, when we feel to our sorrow that it is done already? Surely what we should ask in these cases is that our will may be brought into harmony with God's will, that what He desires to accomplish in us by His chastening may come to pass at once. To pray for this is perfectly right, and this desire is included in the petition, "Thy will be done." But it is not the direct meaning of the words. Are we to use a prayer which speaks *of the future*, only when we are mourning over *the past?*

Two remarkable examples in the New Testament will show the true place of this prayer. Our Saviour Himself prayed it three times over in Gethsemane. But what need was there that *He* should pray thus? Did He pray because of what had befallen Him already, or in view of what was to come? There was indeed the greatest necessity for prayer. The most important crisis in the history of our world was close at hand. The salvation of mankind was at stake, and on Him alone, on JESUS of Nazareth, it depended whether the world was lost or won.

The last act of a life, the sum of which was "To do Thy will, O God," was before Him. Hitherto His obedience had been perfect; every opportunity had been used, every attack repelled or turned aside. There remained only the final struggle. It was the Father's will that JESUS CHRIST should suffer alone for the sin of the whole world, that He should take the world's guilt and the world's punishment as His own, and bear the uttermost wrath of heaven in the face of the malice of united hell.

This was the path open before our Saviour. By this way He must pass, through this He must go without a spot of sin. One false step would have cast the world into perdition. As yet there were no apparent signs of the storm. No enemies were visible. Even the traitor was not yet there. At this moment, when there was still a short calm before that awful tempest, Jesus knelt and prayed once, twice, and again, more and more earnestly, with strong crying and tears, in agony, and with great drops of blood falling down to the ground, and the substance of His prayer was this:—"O my Father, if this cup may not pass away from Me except I drink it, Thy will be done." Can we say that our Lord was not thinking of the future but only of the past? No! "Thy will be done" is of tenfold more value at the entrance of the valley of trouble, than when we have come out. By this prayer our Lord obtained the strength to support His manhood through the utmost suffering that man can have to bear. God's will was done in Him, by Him, and upon Him, and to that will every soul owes his holiness who is numbered with God's saints in glory everlasting.

After this wonderful example of our Saviour, it is scarcely needful to consult the disciples at Cæsarea, the friends of St. Paul. When we see the Spirit of the Master so clearly, can we learn much more from the conduct of the servants? Their testimony points the same way. (Acts xxi. 8–14.) St. Paul had been sent to the poor saints at Jerusalem with a contribution, and he was not to be hindered from fulfilling his business by the prospect of bonds and afflictions. When his companions saw that though their tears might break Paul's heart, they could not alter his purpose, they ceased, saying, "The will of the Lord be done." This was no sullen consent to troubles that were already upon them, but a brave and steadfast appeal to God for strength to stand fast in trials yet to come.

The prayer, "Thy will be done," is meant to strengthen us for what is before us, more than to reconcile us to that which lies behind. But we need not confine the prayer to times of suffering. Suffering is not an essential part of the will of God for us. "He doth not afflict *willingly* nor grieve the children of men." The malice of our adversary the devil, and those things in us which incline to the devil's side, are the cause of all that we suffer in following out the will of God. The prayer that we may do God's will belongs to times of health no less than times of sickness, times of prosperity as well as times when the weakness of our mortal nature is the chief thing before our eyes.

Further, we ask not merely that we may do God's will, but that His will may be *done*.

The word *done* in this passage is not the word used in St. Matt. xii. 50—"Whosoever shall *do the will* of My Father"—but a far larger word. Let Thy will *be brought to pass* in all places and by all means on earth, in the hearts of believing men, and also by the counsels of the wicked; by the ministry of angels as well as by the well-doing of the saints; by the malice of the devil as well as through the Saviour's love; by all the powers of nature, by everything that moves and works on earth. By everything that has a beginning, and a progress, and an end, let one thing be brought to pass, and let that one thing be the will of the Father which is in heaven.

In this larger sense what are we to understand by the will of God? For it may be said that all things that are, are by His will. "The Lord hath made all things for Himself, yea, even the wicked for the day of evil" (Prov. xvi. 4). And according to the testimony of heaven, all things that are, are because God wills them so to be, "Thou hast created all things, and for Thy pleasure (will) they are, and were created" (Rev. iv. 11). But though God's will is always done, yet some ways of doing it are put before us as being more for His glory than others. According to His own word, nothing is so entirely agreeable to His will on earth as when man changes an evil will for a good one, when one who has been foremost in all works of enmity and hatred against God, is won over to do Him reasonable service. Let us observe the passage in 1 Tim. ii. 4, "God wills all men to be saved, and to come to the knowledge of the truth." And the Old Testament is just as clear: "As I live, saith the Lord God, I have no pleasure in the death of the wicked" (Ezek. xxxiii. 2). He makes no exception. The thing that He desires upon earth is, that all men should have salvation from sin, that is, from opposition to Himself. But He desires this end to be brought about in the way which He has Himself provided, the way that glorifies His Son. In Eph. i. 9, 10, we find that His will is "to sum up all things in Christ," making the universe, as it were, one organised body, of which Christ is the head. When we speak of doing God's will on earth we speak of the salvation of man through Christ and into Christ. And further, if we are in Christ, the will of God is declared to be "our sanctification;" "That every one of us should know how to possess his vessel" (that is, to keep his body) "in sanctification and honour" (1 Thess. iv. 3). It is God's will that we should be "perfect in every good work" (Heb. xiii. 21);

"that with well-doing we should put to silence the ignorance of foolish men" (1 Pet. ii. 15); that living in Christ, and by Christ, and like Christ, we should receive the bounty of our God, and walking always in the light of His countenance, should "in everything give thanks" (1 Thess. v. 18).

There is one most important thing in which God's will is again and again asserted. Those that receive Christ, and receiving Him have "power to become the sons of God," owe their lives to His will. Of these children of God a most comforting word is said, which applies to them immediately upon their birth (St. Matt. xviii. 14). "There is no will before your Father which is in heaven that one of these little ones should perish." And it follows them to the end. It is God's will that every one which seeth the Son and believeth upon Him should both have everlasting life here, and be raised up again at the last day (St. John vi. 39, 40). All the powers of darkness may combine to hinder it, but the will of God is against them; so that when we use this prayer, "Thy will be done," we pray for the salvation of all mankind. We pray that all things on earth may be brought into subjection to Jesus Christ. We pray that those persons who are in Christ may be sanctified, made perfect in every good work, and give God thanks in everything. And finally, we pray that every soul who is in Christ, even the veriest babe, may be kept henceforward until the resurrection. What a comfort for a doubting believer! The whole Church of God, every time it makes use of the Lord's Prayer, prays for his endurance unto the end, for his happiness at the resurrection. The prayer is according to the will of God, for it is only because He wills it that we can ask it. "If we ask anything according to His will, He heareth us; and if we know that He hears us, whatsoever we ask, we know that we have the petitions that we desired of Him" (1 John v. 14, 15). Need we add that the greater prayer includes the less: and that all good things which are contained in the good pleasure of God's good will to His children are asked in these words: "For the Lord God is a sun and shield. The Lord will give grace and glory, and no good thing will He withhold from them that walk uprightly." Truly, we do not ask for sorrow when we pray, "Thy will be done."

The Three First Petitions.

—o—

WE have already observed that there are three petitions in the Lord's Prayer which concern more especially the things of God: "Hallowed be Thy name, Thy Kingdom come, Thy will be done, on earth as it is in heaven."

There seems little reason to doubt that in these three petitions, as in many other passages of Holy Scripture, there is a reference to the three Persons of the Godhead—the Father, the Son, and the Holy Ghost. Thus, when we say, Hallowed be Thy name, we understand that our Saviour has taught us that God will be known as a Holy Father throughout the world. It is not easy to realise at the same time God's holiness and His love. Those who dwell much upon the one are apt to forget the other. Some are so occupied with thoughts of His holy law and their own shortcomings, that they can hardly bring themselves to think of Him except as an offended lawgiver. He does not seem like a Father to them. Others, again, are so full of their own notions of His universal goodness, that they will have Him to be the Father of all men, whether holy or unholy; so that all alike shall come into His presence whatever their lives have been; and men may live as they please without fear of consequences, or at least without the fear of being finally lost. Against both these mistakes the Lord Jesus teaches us to pray. We ask that God may be known by all men as their Father, and yet that His name may be accounted holy, as it really is. "Holy Father" was one of the names which our Saviour used in His parting prayer for us (St. John xvii. 11). "Holy Father, keep through Thine own name those whom Thou hast given Me, that they may be one, as we are." When all men can pray to a Holy Father and acknowledge equally His spotless holiness and His parental love, then the prayer will be answered, "Hallowed be Thy name."

And as the first petition refers to the person of the Father, so we may take the second in relation to the Son: "Thy kingdom come." For it is Christ's kingdom that we expect to see established over the world in which we live. Before the kingdom of the Father we look for the kingdom of the Son. God has declared that He will put all things under the feet of Jesus. He is that "man of noble birth who went into a far country, to receive for Himself a kingdom and to return" (St. Luke xix. 12). When He comes again He will come in His kingdom. The Lord grant us that we may find mercy of Him in that day.

And the third petition of the Lord's Prayer may well remind us of the Holy Spirit. Without that Spirit it is impossible to do God's will. When the Evil One came to our first parents in Paradise, where all around them was in their favour, they fell at the first assault. When he came to the Holy One in the wilderness after forty days and forty nights of loneliness, he entirely failed. Why? "Jesus, *being full of the Holy Ghost*, returned from Jordan, and was *led by the Spirit* into the wilderness." And why are we taught concerning the law of God, which is the expression of His will, that "the letter killeth, but the Spirit giveth life?" Because without the Spirit no man can even understand, much less keep the letter of the law. "Thy commandment is exceeding broad." When it reaches to the thoughts and intents of the heart, and commands obedience even in our wishes and imaginations, what can we do? As long as God gave men only "the letter," the law was but "the ministration of death." "The Spirit giveth life." And this "spirit" is not only the meaning, nor merely the scope and intention, of the law. The meaning of the law will no more give life to fallen humanity than the words. The difficulty of keeping the ten commandments is not lessened by reading the sermon on the mount. The Holy Spirit alone can bring the mind of God into man's heart, showing him what God's law is, and enabling him to love it. "I will run the way of Thy commandments, when Thou hast set my heart at liberty." And therefore, when we pray that God's will may be done *in us*, we ask what cannot be without the Holy Spirit's abiding presence in our hearts. And thus this third petition touches the question of our sanctification more closely than anything else. If there is one place in man where the root of ungodliness seems to have gone deepest, it is his will. How many times we might do right and might avoid sin if only we *would* do it. Our own will is a thing very near and dear to us all. We do not often find ourselves inclined to contradict the other petitions in the Lord's Prayer, but this petition must have its negative as well as its positive side. Our blessed Lord Himself prayed, "*Not as I will*, but as Thou wilt: *not My will*, but Thine be done." This is the prayer that most reminds us of our weakness and ignorance; and makes most demands upon our patience, on our faith in God as a Father, and our trust in our Father's love. And yet, exacting as this petition seems to be, we are required to make it before we ask anything for ourselves. According to the order of the Lord's Prayer, we may not ask for daily bread, for forgiveness of trespasses, or for deliverance from evil, until we have first said, "Thy will be done." We are not our own, we belong to our Father in heaven, and if we do not mean to obey Him, what right have we to exist, or to ask His permission to live? But, on the other hand, the most valuable gift that we have is our will. God might have given us more strength or beauty, more skill or power of motion, more glory and grandeur in every other way; but nothing else that He could have given would make up for the loss of our will—the one thing which He has given that makes this prayer so difficult, but without which it would be meaningless to say, "Thy will be done." The greatest glory that we can have is to be able, of our own free choice, to please the God who made us; to choose to do His will, even though we can choose otherwise, because we believe that He is wiser than ourselves. But what can be a greater disgrace than to say to our Maker, "Not Thy will but my will;" to say, in fact, "I, with the little power and knowledge that He has given me, know better than He does, though He made the sight and hearing, the mind and judgment, the affection and feeling without which I cannot choose at all." We can easily see that this will of ours embraces the whole mystery of what shall become of us in another world. If we are to remain what we now are, beings with a will of our own, and that will is not taught and trained to act always in submission to the will of Him who made us,—if we have not learnt to choose obedience rather than wilfulness by the time our learning days are over,—what can become of us except to be shut out from the presence of our God? Let us thank God that He sent His Son in our nature to show us how to be obedient, to create a power of obedience in us and give a spirit of obedience to us, so that it is possible, through our Lord Jesus, for sinful man to say under the greatest pressure: "*Not as I will*, but as Thou wilt: *not My will*, but Thine be done."

We have seen how these three petitions bring to mind the three Persons of the glorious Godhead. But are they not all addressed to One who is called "Our Father?" Is not the name that we desire to hallow the name of our Father, the kingdom that is to come the kingdom of our Father, the will that is to be done the will of our Father, and the Holy Spirit that does it the Spirit of our Father? Certainly it is. And here let us notice that in the ages to come it is revealed by the New Testament that the children of God will be brought much nearer to their Father than they can at present understand. As yet "no man hath seen God at any time." Jesus Christ alone has "declared Him." And for our part, *we* have not yet seen the Lord Jesus. We desire to see Him. And if we are His we shall see Him and be like Him. But as yet we can only know Him by the presence of the Holy Spirit in our hearts. God the Father is known only through God the Son. And *we* know God the Son only by God the Holy Spirit. But it will not be so always. This knowledge of God is like a ladder set on earth whose top reaches to heaven. And God's children shall climb from step to step, and from strength to strength, until they come to the God of glory. JEHOVAH alone stands above this ladder, and when we reach the top, we shall see Him that is there.

There is a name in the New Testament which we generally apply to God the Son, but it need not belong to Him only. In Rev. i. 4, 5, we read thus: "Grace be unto you, and peace, from Him which is, and which was, and which is to come; and from the seven Spirits which are before His throne; And from Jesus Christ, who is the faithful Witness, and the first begotten of the dead, and the Prince of the kings of the earth. Unto Him that loved us, and washed us from our sins in His own blood, and hath made us kings and priests unto God and His Father; to Him be glory and dominion for ever and ever. Amen." This appears to be a blessing in the name of the Holy Trinity. It is from Jesus Christ, the second Person, and "from the seven Spirits before His throne." In these we recognise the presence of the Holy Ghost, the third Person.

The first name of all would thus appear to belong to our Father—the name "which is, and which was, and which is to *come.*" If that be indeed a name of God the Father, there is such a thing as the *coming* of the Father. It is not merely that He is, and was, and is to *be*, but that He "is to *come.*" The title which is in many places applied to Christ to signify His coming, is here applied to the Father. Thus we are led to believe that He will COME ALSO; that, as we read in 1 Cor. xv., Christ shall deliver up the kingdom to God, even the Father; and the Father shall be with us, and spread His tabernacle with us Himself. Something of this kind seems to be suggested in the end of the book of Revelation, where we read of *one* throne only in the golden city, the throne of God and of the Lamb; one temple only, the Lord God Almighty and the Lamb. "Behold," it is said, "the tabernacle of *God* is with men," . . . "God *Himself* shall be with them." "He that overcometh shall inherit these things, and I will be his *God*, and he shall be My son."

Something of this kind was also foreshadowed in the words of our Saviour, that "the righteous shall shine forth as the sun in the *Kingdom of their Father.*" "Who hath ears to hear, let him hear."

Give us this day (day by day) our daily Bread.

—o—

WE now come to that portion of the Lord's Prayer which more directly refers to ourselves. And our first request reminds us of our own mortality. When we think of the things of our Father—His name, His kingdom, and His will—we may let our thoughts about the future take what range they will. We may let them travel onward to the time when "the earth shall be full of the knowledge of the Lord, as the waters cover the sea." As regards the glory of God, our aspirations need have no limit in time, or in the whole breadth of the world. But when we pray for ourselves, our ambition must be severely and strictly restrained. Our time is to-day only. Our wants are limited by the Lord's Prayer to daily bread.

From this point we may obtain a glimpse of His mind who first conceived the prayer. It was His meat and drink to do the will of Him that sent Him. For Himself He asked sufficient strength and support to be able to do that. When shall we learn to take the same view of life as simply and naturally as our Lord? When shall we recognise the fact that we are not our own, that we live for Him who made us, and that to live for ourselves is as much robbery as for a servant to take his master's time and property and spend it all upon his own pleasure? No one who does not live to seek God's Kingdom, by doing his daily work for the glory of God, can really enter into the spirit of this prayer. All the self-indulgent theories of life, the making our own way, and securing our own ease and comfort, with the hope that some day or other we may have time to think of God, all this kind of thing is quietly put aside by the Lord's Prayer: "Hallowed be Thy name, Thy kingdom come, Thy will be done, on earth as it is in heaven." And while we are endeavouring to hallow that name, to extend that kingdom, and to do that will, leave us not unsupported. "Give us this day our daily bread."

But the limitation of this prayer in respect of time is no less striking than its limitation of the objects which we may pursue. For *to-day* only we ask. It is true that there is some further concession to human anxiety in the other version of the prayer (in St. Luke xi). But, as we generally use the words, "*to-day*" is the limit of our prayer. For we are ourselves creatures of to-day. "All flesh is grass, and all the glory of man as the flower of the grass"—"the grass of the field which *to-day* is, and to-morrow is cast into the oven." It is for to-day that God requires our services. "Son, go work *to-day* in My vineyard." "*To-day*, if ye will hear His voice, harden not your hearts." It may be that to-morrow ye will hear it no more. It is not merely that we cannot say to our soul, "Soul, thou hast much goods laid up for *many years*." We cannot even calculate on another day. "Go to now, ye that say, To-day *and to-morrow* we will go into such a city, and continue there a year, and buy and sell and get gain." You talk of a *year*, but you "know not what shall be on the *morrow*. For what is your life? It is even as a vapour that appeareth for a little time, and then vanisheth away." Say then "to-day" I will do so and so if you will, but not "to-day and to-morrow." You cannot be sure of that. "If the Lord will, we shall live;" but "Boast not thyself of to-morrow, for thou knowest not what a day"—the very day that is now coming on—"thou knowest not what to-day may bring forth."

It is comparatively easy to draw a lesson from this petition against boasting of our prospects in life. But there is another lesson of an opposite kind to be drawn from it which takes much longer to learn, and that is a lesson against *care*. We cannot but associate with this petition our Lord's precept to bear no anxiety for the morrow, and in respect of what may happen *then* (but not to-day) not to be "of doubtful mind." How wonderfully the principle of this petition was enforced upon Israel in the wilderness, when for forty years they were fed with manna! And yet they never had to-morrow's food in the house to-day, except on the eve of the Sabbath. To lay up manna was not only forbidden, it was impossible, except for the Sabbath-day. "It bred worms and stank," teaching by its very decay the same lesson which our Saviour has put into words for us: "Lay not up for yourselves treasures upon earth, where moth and rust disfigure, and where thieves break through and steal. But lay up for yourselves treasures in heaven," where you shall find them "an inheritance incorruptible and undefiled" on the day of rest that "remaineth for the people of God."

But there are some minds to whom preparation for the morrow seems to be really part of the duty of to-day. And it is impossible to forget the duty of providing, if not for self, at least for those who may be dependent upon others, when we can go out and gather for them no more. A concession is certainly made to this lawful forethought in the language of the petition which we are considering in St. Luke xi. 3. *There* it is "give us *day by day* our daily bread." This is the first petition in the prayer which admits any variation. And the change is no doubt meant to instruct us.

The request worded in St. Matthew is precise: "Give us," *i.e.*, give now, at this particular time, for this very day, "our daily bread." The morrow is left absolutely out of sight.* We do not even pray for it

* I do not forget the true derivation of the Greek word for "daily," as maintained by modern scholars. No doubt that word *ep-iousios* is derived from *ep-iousa*. *Ep-iousa* occurs several times in the Acts of the Apostles, and means *the ensuing day*. *Ep-iousios*, when applied to bread, means bread for the *day that is coming on*. But it would not be fair to say that "Give us this day our daily bread" means, "Give us to-day the bread that we shall need to-morrow." We may very properly remind ourselves that in Holy Scripture the evening and the morning make the day. To-morrow begins when to-day's sun goes

there. But forasmuch as our heavenly Father knew that for some of us, the only possible way to avoid care for the morrow would be prayer for it, He has also taught us by our Saviour a petition that comprises the whole of our earthly life. This we find in St. Luke—the gospel of our Lord's Humanity, when it is written, "give us," *i.e.*, not for once only, but give, and continue to give us, "day by day" as the time continues, "our daily bread."

This is not to be made an excuse for extravagance and needless luxury, but it at least includes as much as the prayer of Agur in Proverbs (chap. xxx. 7–9): "Two things have I required of Thee; deny me them not before I die: remove far from me vanity and lies: give me neither poverty nor riches; feed me with food convenient for me: lest I be full, and deny Thee, and say, Who is the Lord? or lest I be poor, and steal, and take the name of my God in vain." This, which is in effect a prayer to be kept from sin, is certainly included in the petitions that may be used. And so in the vow of Jacob (Gen. xxviii. 20, 21): "If

down. And thus, if we say the Lord's Prayer in the morning, "the bread of the day that is coming on" means to-day's provision. If we say it at night, it means to-morrow's provision. But does it therefore contradict the precept that we should "take no anxiety for the morrow?" Surely not. On the contrary, it enables us before we slumber to "cast all our care upon Him who cares for us." We "sleep and rise, night and day," and His corn springs and grows up, we know not how. But knowing that it does, we intrust Him with the wants of to-morrow, in order that we may rest without care to-night. We lie down under the shadow of His wings who will not slumber, knowing that before the sun awakes us, He will have made provision for the morrow's need. We shall not find Him unprepared, when we rise up in the morning, and ask Him for our daily bread.

God will be with me, and keep me in this way that I go, and will give me bread to eat and raiment to put on, so that I come again to my father's house in peace, then shall the Lord be my God." To this extent, and for this purpose, and in this kind of spirit, we may pray for the care of God over our bodily necessities for the *whole* of life. Only we must learn "in whatsoever state we are, having food and raiment, therewith to be content."

But the two forms of this petition in St. Matthew and St. Luke do not really differ after all. The petition as it is in St. Matthew is framed for a single day. In St. Luke we have the same prayer, only so worded as to include the whole life. God would not have given us the power to look forward, if He did not mean that we should commit our prospects and anticipations, as well as our present troubles, to Him. There is no view of the future so clear, or so calm, or so satisfactory, as that view which we may obtain in God's sanctuary, or in private, at our Father's throne of grace. Now let us glance at the real reason why we may be kept from all care for the morrow; why we must "be content with such things as we have." It is because He hath said, "I will never leave thee, nor forsake thee" (Heb. xiii. 5). "*He* hath said?" Who? The God of Israel, the God of Abraham, and Isaac, and Jacob. It is not often that *He* is thus introduced in the New Testament without a name. But *when* did He say this? The answer is very beautiful. It really is not an exact quotation from any one passage, but a reference to three, belonging to three remarkable periods of the history of the people of God. First, it was said to Jacob, the "Syrian ready to perish," when he went out alone from his father's house to pass over Jordan with his staff only. When he lay on the ground at Bethel with the stones of that place for his pillow, and saw the ladder set on the earth, whose top reached to heaven, behold the Lord stood above it and said to that poor and lonely traveller, "I am Jehovah, the God of Abraham thy father, and the God of Isaac: the land whereon thou liest, to thee will I give it, and to thy seed; and thy seed shall be as the dust of the earth, and thou shalt spread abroad to the west, and to the east, and to the north, and to the south: and in thee and in thy seed shall all the families of the earth be blessed. And, behold, I am with thee, and will keep thee in all places whither thou goest, and will bring thee again into this land; for I WILL NOT LEAVE THEE, until I have done that which I have spoken to thee of" (Gen. xxviii. 13–15).

That saying, "I will not leave thee," is the source of the last clause of the promise, "I will not forsake thee." We cannot now even glance at the chief incidents of Jacob's long and chequered life. But God was with him. We have it from his own lips on his deathbed, "The God that has been and is my Shepherd all my life long unto this day, the Angel that redeemeth me from all evil, bless the lads" (Gen. xlviii. 15, 16).

And the promise was given to Joshua in view of his great work of leading Israel into the promised land: "There shall not a man be able to stand before thee all the days of thy life: as I was with Moses, so I will be with thee: I WILL NOT FAIL THEE, nor forsake thee" (Josh. i. 5). Here we get the first clause of the promise. We cannot now review the life of Joshua either, but we will remind ourselves how at the close of his work it is written, "There failed not ought of any good thing which the Lord had spoken unto the house of Israel; all came to pass." And Joshua resolved to the very last for himself and for that posterity whose names are only "written in heaven," that, "As for me and for my house, we will serve the Lord"* (Josh. xxiv. 15).

And, thirdly, it was David's exhortation to Solomon when about to complete the establishment of the throne of glory in the promised land, when the temple and palace of God's kingdom were to be built. "David said to Solomon, his son, be strong and of good courage and do it; fear not nor be dismayed; for the Lord God, even my God, will be with thee; He will not *fail thee nor forsake* thee, until thou hast finished all the work for the service of the house of the Lord." Thus the promise came to the Hebrews backed by all these names and

* For Joshua himself the service of Jehovah on earth was nearly over. He pledges his "house" to the same service. What is known of his family? It is a singular fact that no descendant of the Great Conqueror, no member of his household, is named in the Bible. In the genealogies of Ephraim in 1 Chron. vii., Joshua's name is the last in his own line, v. 27. I cannot but regard the silence of Scripture under this head as profoundly significant. It is one more analogy between the Joshua of the Old Testament and His great Antitype in the Gospel. "*Whose house are we*, if we hold fast the confidence and the rejoicing of the hope firm unto the end" (Heb. iii. 6). The house of Joshua embraces all the faithful servants of the Lord.

histories. It was a promise to pay, endorsed with the names of largest experience in their history—Jacob, and Joshua, and Solomon—yes, and Moses and David too; for Moses had said it to Joshua in his lifetime before Jehovah Himself said it after Moses' death. All these, moreover, are recognised types of Christ. Jacob, Joshua, and Solomon are three peculiarly significant types, for they stand at the beginning and the middle and the end of Israel's national glory. Jacob, the father of the twelve patriarchs; Joshua, the founder of the twelve tribes in Canaan; and Solomon, who completed the city which was peopled by all Israel, and has a gate for every tribe,—the city that "is at unity in itself, whither the tribes go up, even the tribes of the Lord." Between these three men,—Jacob at Bethel, Joshua at the entrance of the land of promise, and "Solomon in all his glory,"—every step and stage of the Christian pilgrimage is set forth. And in all alike there is the promise, "I will never leave thee, nor forsake thee."

No one will ever know how true God's word is until he casts his whole weight upon it. "*He hath said,*" who "is not a man that He should lie, or the son of man that He should repent." "Hath He said and shall He not do it; hath He spoken and shall He not make it good?"

We must notice two things more about our "daily bread." The word used is peculiar, and it is thought that it was coined for the purpose, being found only here and in the Lord's Prayer in St. Luke. There seems to be no room for doubt that it means bread for the day that is coming on. That daily bread can be understood spiritually as well as naturally, who can doubt?* God our Father seeks true worshippers to worship Him. And true worshippers may surely ask for true bread. And the true bread is what our Father gives from heaven. "The bread of God is He which cometh down from heaven and giveth life unto the world." "Give us this day our daily bread," is certainly a prayer for the Holy Spirit, when it is rightly used and understood. The Holy Spirit is Christ's representative on earth. And Christ is the Living Bread.

We may also observe that we ask for *bread*. Not the food of unfallen man in Paradise, but the food appointed for him to win by labour after the Fall.

Let no one think that he can live in idleness, and yet hope to be supported by the Lord's Prayer. "In the sweat of thy face shalt thou eat *bread* until thou return unto the ground." It implies our own willingness to labour when we ask for daily bread. That which is not earned by honest labour, is not obtained according to God's ordinance, is not really *Bread*. And in that Christ is called "the true bread from heaven," let us remember the labour that it cost Him to give life to the world. Remember that "Bread corn is bruised," and "He was bruised for our iniquities." As the corn of wheat falls into the ground and dies, that it may not abide alone, so did our Saviour *die*, that He might arise again, to be the first fruits of them that slept." Our life is the fruit of His labour. "We being many are one *bread* and

* There seems to be no solid foundation for the view that it means "supersubstantial," according to the Latin version of the prayer.

one body in Him, for we are all partakers of that one bread." Thus our daily bread speaks to us both of the Fall and also of redemption, and it has been chosen to be the sign of that body wherein Christ bare our sins upon the tree. We do not find *bread* spoken of as the food of heaven. "As often as ye eat this bread and drink this cup ye do shew the Lord's death *till He come*." But when He comes, labour as connected with the curse will be over. The word spoken in connection with the New Jerusalem, that not only death and sorrow and crying shall have an end for ever, but "neither shall there be any more *pain*,"* marks the cessation of hard labour, such as God ordained for Adam, for evermore. "To him that overcometh will I give to eat of the hidden manna and of the tree of life," is our Lord's promise. There we return to the food of Paradise once more. And we read that in the midst of the street of that city—where man's life shall no more be counted by the day, "for there shall be no night there,"—"in the midst of the street of it, and on either side the river, was there the tree of life, which bare twelve manner of fruits, and yielded her fruit every month, and the leaves of the tree were for the healing of the nations. And there shall be no more curse." The decree, that in the sweat of his face man shall eat bread, will then have been accomplished; and it may well be that in that day there will be no need to use this petition any longer, "Give us this day our *daily bread*."

* In Greek *ponos*, *i.e.*, the toil of the needy.

Forgive us our Debts, as we forgive our Debtors.

——o——

IN this sentence we find the first open and direct mention of *sin* which occurs in the Lord's Prayer. Not that the earlier petitions are constructed without reference to sin. There would be no need to pray that God's name may be hallowed, if it *were* hallowed; or, that His will may be done on earth, if it were done without question now. The three first petitions all imply that we live in the realms of disobedience as regards this present world. But in this petition that general state of disobedience is noticed as extending to ourselves. Every individual who makes use of this prayer must confess himself a sinner. "Forgive us our debts," or as it is in St. Luke, "Forgive us our *sins*," is a prayer for no one but a sinner. On this account, there have been some who objected to use the prayer. If the objection presents itself to any of our readers, it may be well to remember that we shall probably have debts as long as we have debtors. We cannot expect other people to allow that they have no neglect or offence to charge against us until we can say that we meet with no offence ourselves. No man can say that he is without sin, until he has heard what his neighbours may have against him. As long as there is a single complaint that they can establish, he cannot claim to be perfect in the sight of God. And as for the doctrine that we are without sin when we are in Christ, because "God hath not beheld iniquity in Jacob, neither seen perverseness in Israel," and does not impute iniquity to those that are united to Jesus Christ by faith—it were well if all understood and accepted it indeed, and a blessed truth it is, but—it does not alter the fact, that "If we say that we have no sin we deceive ourselves."

On the night of the last supper, when our Lord washed His disciples' feet, He said to Simon Peter, "If I wash thee not thou hast no part with me." Unless He washes us daily from the pollutions that we contract in our daily pilgrimage, we have no part with Him; we cease to be partakers of Christ, "the Lord who healeth us." He is our Healer, not for one day only, but every day, till the body of sin is destroyed, and we "awake after His likeness." We need not dwell longer on the opinion of those who abstain from using the Lord's Prayer because it contains a petition for the forgiveness of sins. Let *us* rather take it as a proof of the "faithful saying, and worthy of all acceptation, that Christ Jesus came into the world to save *sinners*."

It did not make Him forsake the work of saving us, even when He knew that every day of our lives until the last day we should be sinners still.

As often as we ask for daily bread, so often did He know that we must ask forgiveness. And yet, with all this, "He sent redemption unto His people, and commanded His covenant for ever, Holy and Reverend is His Name."*

We may notice now that of all the petitions in the Lord's Prayer this was the only one on which our Saviour added any comment when He first delivered it. As soon as the prayer is concluded, we find Him explaining this portion (St. Matt. vi. 14, 15): "For if ye forgive men their trespasses, your heavenly Father will also forgive you: But if ye forgive not

* If this page should meet the eye of any one who is really perplexed by the arguments against the use of the Lord's Prayer, the following observations may be of service :—

The Lord's Prayer stands part of the Sermon on the Mount. In this sermon our Lord distinctly ordained the use of the prayer. "When ye pray, say, Our Father;" and at the close of the sermon He said, "Whosoever heareth these sayings of mine and doeth them not, shall be likened unto a foolish man, who built his house upon the sand." This is our Lord's own judgment upon those who neglect His orders. But, it is said, the Sermon on the Mount was delivered before Pentecost, and belongs therefore to the Jewish dispensation. The argument proves too much. Every word that our Lord spoke in the Gospels was spoken before Pentecost, and belongs, thus far, to the Jewish dispensation. Are we therefore to correct the Gospels by the Epistles, and set the words of the disciples above the words of the Lord? But, although the words of Christ were spoken before Pentecost, *they were not written till after Pentecost.* And they were written in obedience to the order recorded by St. Matthew, that the disciples should *teach all nations to observe all things whatsoever He had commanded them.* Therefore they wrote the Gospels. If the Sermon on the Mount was superseded, why did St. Matthew write it in the Gospel, with the tremendous sanction with which it closes, and never so much as hint that it is not binding upon us? Those who take upon themselves to make selections from the sayings of our Lord, and obey some and reject others, do in reality set themselves above Him.

men their trespasses, neither will your Father forgive your trespasses." He delivered an entire parable on another occasion to enforce the same lesson. When St. Peter asked, "Lord, how oft shall my brother sin against me, and I forgive him? till seven times? Jesus saith unto him, I say not unto thee, Until seven times: but until seventy times seven" (St. Matt. 18, 21-35). We learn from St. Mark (chap. xi. 25, 26), that the lesson was repeated a third time as the disciples were entering Jerusalem the day after the barren fig-tree was cursed. This time the subject of discourse was faith. He adds, "When ye stand praying, forgive, if ye have ought against any: that your Father also which is in heaven may forgive you your trespasses. But if ye do not forgive, neither will your Father which is in heaven forgive your trespasses."

It would seem from St. Luke (chap. vi. 37), that the same precept was twice repeated in the Sermon on the Mount, for we read, "Judge not, and ye shall not be judged: condemn not, and ye shall not be condemned: *forgive, and ye shall be forgiven.*" One cannot but notice the *fact* that our Saviour has said so much in the Gospel upon this subject.

It has been wisely written,* "Unless an unforgiving temper were an exceedingly common, as well as a most deadly possession, our Lord would never have said so much about it in the Gospel as He does. Unforgivingness must needs be a sin to which every heart is prone,—and which in the case of many

* "Short Sermons for Family Reading," by the Very Rev. J. W. Burgon, Dean of Chichester. *Second Series.* Vol. 2, page 746.

must be even now poisoning the very springs of life. As far as I am aware, the subtle method of this sin is to lurk in a corner of the soul, but *there* to entrench itself and make itself secure."

When we are under no particular pressure or provocation, there is no difficulty in appreciating the justice of the principle. "Forgive, and ye shall be forgiven." But when we are tempted and provoked in any matter that really touches our feelings, it is surprising how hard a matter forgiveness is—how we begin to make exceptions—how eagerly we catch at those other sayings which accompany the direct command to forgive those that wrong us—such as, "If thy brother trespass against thee, rebuke him; and if he *repent*, forgive him." Yes, we say to ourselves, "If he repent. But he has not repented. He is not likely to do so, and so I may hate him as I choose. Not that I wish him any evil—I should be quite satisfied never to see him or hear of him again. I do not think about him if I can help it." This is not what our Lord meant by forgiveness. It certainly is *not* obeying the precept, "Love your enemies, bless them that curse you, do good to them that hate you, and pray for them which despitefully use you, and persecute you; that ye may be the children of your Father which is in heaven: for He maketh His sun to rise on the evil and on the good, and sendeth rain on the just and on the unjust" (St. Matt. v. 44, 45).

To treat enemies as friends in this way is what we do not find it easy to do. There is only one thing that gives us power to obey the commandment; only one kind of knowledge that helps us to understand the rights of the case. That knowledge is a sense of our own obligations to our God and Saviour for His redeeming love, and the power that enables us to put our knowledge in practice is the love of Christ.

Perhaps it may help us to understand the principle of the thing if we notice the peculiar way in which our sins are described in reference to the duty of forgiveness. They are spoken of as "*debts*." It is a pity that in our common version of the Lord's Prayer we have not preserved this allusion, but have substituted the word trespasses. For the idea of *debt* is certainly essential to the view of sin that Christ has presented to us here. Sin is an unpaid debt, and a sinner is an insolvent debtor. From this view of the thing one conclusion follows immediately: we must forgive others as God forgives us, without insisting upon the discharge of all obligations, or the payment of all that is due. To forgive a debtor is to let him go free, when his debt is still owing, as though he had paid it. We must not forget that all our sins are debts that we still owe to God. Every sin leaves us with something not done, something unpaid which we shall never be able to make up, whatever we may do or pay in time to come. "Forgive us our debts" we pray, and the very word we use implies that the *debt* still remains. And so far as we are concerned, we shall never be able to pay. The word *sin* used in St. Luke xi. involves the same sort of idea. A sin is literally a *miss*—a mistake that cannot be corrected—a lost opportunity that can never be recalled. We are like unjust stewards—we have been wasting our Master's goods. In everything that we do wrong there is more to be taken account of than the positive harm that is done. God looks at what we might have been doing for His service in the time that we wasted, and with the strength and energy that we expended upon sin. God who made us has a right to the use of all our powers at every moment—a right to employ us and direct us as He thinks fit. When we please ourselves, or do the service of the world and the devil, our Master is a loser, not only by the evil that we do, but by the time we spend, and the good we leave undone. Thus we become His debtors—we can never recall the time past, the word spoken, the act done. "God requireth that which is past," and if it was wrong, it will never be recovered. The opportunity is lost beyond recall. Although God graciously accepts the service of His beloved Son instead of our failures, in the assurance that He will one day make faithful servants of us after all, yet on our part there is a failure for the present that is not made up by any repentance or amendment, or confession of sin. Even death, which we call "the debt of nature," does not make amends for our mischief, it only brings our opportunities for evil in this world to an end.

This fact, that we are debtors to God, and hopelessly bankrupt, so to speak, ought to make us think very carefully what right we have to claim our own debts from others. And do we not claim them in every instance when we refuse to forgive? What do all our excuses for hating our enemy really mean but this? If he would only confess that he has done wrong to us; if he would express regret or promise not to offend again, or do something to indicate a change of mind, then we would forgive him. Yes! If the debtor would pay in full, or pay something, or even acknowledge himself a debtor, we could forgive! But that is not our Lord's forgiveness. It was when they had *nothing* to pay that He frankly forgave them both. We must recollect that our tears and prayers, our resolutions and promises, are no *payment* for the opportunities which we have wasted, for the harm which we have done. Repentance may prove that you know you are a debtor; but it does nothing to pay the debt. When we are too eager for acknowledgment and amendment on the part of others, we are not doing as our Lord did to us. "While we were yet *sinners*, Christ died for us." When we were still "*enemies*, we were reconciled to God by the death of His Son," before we had even acknowledged ourselves to be in debt. Can we forgive debts that remain unpaid in full, as God for Christ's sake hath forgiven us? To do this requires a deep conviction of our own utter sinfulness, and of God's redeeming love. This we cannot have except we see Jesus. Accordingly we find that this petition was, when Christ delivered it, quite a new prayer. Other parts of the Lord's Prayer were not altogether different from some of the Old Testament petitions. "Forgive us our trespasses, *as we forgive*," was a petition not used before the coming of our Saviour Christ. Then God gave the example which He expects us to follow. He revealed the great principle of forgiveness which He expects us now to understand, at least sufficiently to put it in practice. We can only do so by putting the Lord Jesus in all His sufferings in the place of our enemies, just as God puts Him in our place, and accepts Him in our stead. The sufferings of our Lord Jesus Christ are the propitiation for our offences against each other, as well as for our sins against God. Jesus Christ is our *peace* in every sense of the word. He is the satisfaction to you and to me for all the shortcomings and offences of our neighbour, as well as for our trangressions against God.

If you ask for proof of this from Holy Scripture, the proof is obvious. For if Jesus Christ be *not* the atonement for any offence that I have committed against my brother, how shall I be forgiven? A breach of my duty to my neighbour is as bad in law as any other crime. "Whosoever shall keep the whole law, and yet offend in one point, he is guilty of all." The latter half of the law is all concerned with offences against mankind. If Jesus Christ is not the satisfaction for these offences, then there is no means provided by which they can be put away. The death of our Lord Jesus must be a satisfaction for man's sins against his neighbour, or else it is not truly a sacrifice for *all* sin.

Then there is another reason. The Prophet Isaiah says in the chapter which speaks of Christ's sufferings (Isa. liii. 10), "Thou shalt make His soul an offering for sin," that is, originally "a trespass-offering." Now, a trespass-offering was distinct and peculiar in its kind. There were five great kinds of offerings provided under the law of Moses: the burnt-offering, the meat-offering, the peace-offering, the sin-offering, and the trespass-offering. Each of these had its own distinct meaning. The object of the trespass-offering was especially to atone for offences against rights or property, whether of God or man. The larger number of trespasses enumerated by the law in Leviticus are trespasses against man. And as all the offerings of the law of Moses were shadows cast by the One great Offering of the body of Jesus Christ, the trespass-offering amongst others was fulfilled in Him. And thus, when His soul was made *a trespass-offering*, He atoned for our offences against each other as well as for our transgressions against God. Observe the cases of trespass indicated in Lev. vi. 1, 2: "If a soul sin and commit a trespass against the Lord, and lie unto his neighbour in that which was delivered him to keep, or in fellowship, or in a thing taken away by violence, or hath deceived his neighbour; or have found that which was lost, and lieth concerning it, and sweareth falsely; in any of all these that a man doeth, sinning therein." All wrong done in fellowship, all unfair dealings of every sort between man and man, are included under this head. Restitution is indeed commanded and ought to be made, but the *guilt* of the sin is taken away by the Great Trespass-Offering. Until the accepted time is over, God does not impute the trespass; and we must not impute it while He does not. This is the love of our Heavenly Father, a love that "imputeth not the evil" which He knows to exist. There is therefore only one thing for us to do with all sin that troubles us; whether it is the wrong dealing of our neighbours, or the wickedness of our own hearts, we must take it to the Cross of Jesus Christ. When the thought of the unkindness that we have suffered comes upon us, we should turn our minds and memories upon Jesus Christ. *He* has taken all the sin of unkindness upon Himself. He was wounded for those transgressions. He was bruised for those iniquities. The punishment which our enemies deserve for their ill-treatment of us was all borne by Him. We must not avenge ourselves upon them, for Christ hath once suffered for their sinfulness, "the just for the unjust," to make peace with God and peace with man. It therefore comes to this. You cannot impute iniquity to your neighbour without ignoring and practically denying the fact that this very iniquity has once already been imputed to Jesus Christ. God made Him to be sin for us, and laid the curse of the law upon Him, that blessing instead of cursing might be the portion of every man. This view of our neighbour's trespasses is not a view which we may accept or reject at pleasure. It is not theory, with which we may entertain ourselves, but a solemn truth and a binding precept, enforced upon us under the most tremendous penalties, which we can only neglect at the utmost peril. It is absolutely stated in the gospel, that if we do not forgive men their trespasses, our Heavenly Father will not forgive us. We need not repeat the story of the unmerciful servant, who was cast into prison because he would not have compassion on his fellow-servant, as the Lord had pity on him. But it will be well to remember the end of the story. "His Lord was wroth, and delivered him to the tormentors till he should pay all that was due unto him." And that "*all*" was a terrible sum. The amount for which he seized his fellow-servant was 100 pence, a sum that represented about three months' wages of a labouring man. But the debt of the unmerciful servant to his master was 10,000 talents, a sum that could not be earned by ordinary labour in 150,000 years! Nor does this suggest a limit; for it does not appear certain that in prison a slave could really earn anything.

And long before he could begin to make any impression upon such a sum as that, his life and his labour would have ceased for ever. But we dare not forget the moral. "So likewise," said our compassionate Saviour, "so likewise shall my Heavenly Father do also unto you, if ye from your hearts forgive not every one his brother their trespasses." Is it not easy to see the reason of this? What can be more reasonable? He who will not allow the atonement of Jesus Christ for others shall not have the benefit for himself. And let us never forget, that to impute to our brother the evil for which Christ died, is in reality to refuse the atonement of Jesus Christ! This is what makes an unforgiving temper unpardonable. If we cannot forgive our brethren, it is clear that we have never truly apprehended the death of Jesus Christ for all sin.

Not to be able to forgive arises either from not understanding or not receiving the true doctrine of forgiveness, that it is *for Jesus Christ's sake.* And it must not make any *internal* difference to our forgiveness of an offending brother whether he repent or no. For the present, God regards even unrepenting sinners, not with anger, but with mercy. "God was in Christ reconciling the world (not only believers) unto Himself, not imputing their trespasses unto them." It is not every one that repents and believes the forgiving love of God. But still, for the time present, God does not impute any trespasses, either to repentant or unrepentant sinners. For "now is the accepted time, now is the day of salvation." It is still the great day of atonement. The High Priest is within the vail, wearing the marks of the sacrifice. And until He comes out again, it is a day of amnesty, an offer of full pardon to every rebel who will lay down his arms and come in. And as with the Father, so with the children. As God does not impute trespasses, so we must not impute them. To-day is sacred to the love that "imputeth not the evil" that it sees and hears. I know that this is not the manner of men, or according to human reasoning. But it is the love of God. And nothing will give us this love except the Holy Spirit dwelling in us. "The fruit of the Spirit is love." God does not wait until we do right that He may forgive us. He forgives us that we may love Him, and learn His ways. If I might receive whatever I asked in this matter, I would ask for you, and for myself, and for all Christians, that whenever the provoking words, and looks, and acts of any one of our fellow-creatures are strongly present to memory or to sense, the impression of this provocation might be hidden by another picture rising before us in its stead.

And *that* picture is more than human hand can draw. It is the picture of Him whose "visage was so marred more than any man, and His form more than the sons of men;" who "gave His back to the smiters, and His cheeks to them that plucked off the hair;" who "hid not His face from shame and spitting;" "who His own self bare our sins in his own body on the tree;" and on whom "Jehovah laid the iniquity of us all."

And with this picture I would ask to realise that the neglect, the treachery, the insults, the blows, the cruelties and pangs of death which are there represented, were borne for the sake of that man or that woman with whom I am tempted at the time to be angry:—that this suffering was the punishment of their wrong-doing; that the meek and unresisting Sufferer is intreating me to accept of His punishment as a satisfaction for their trespasses, while He asks God to accept it as a satisfaction for mine.

If *this* picture could but fill our minds and memories at all times when we feel aggrieved by our fellow-sinners, I think it would be easier to forget our injuries, to forego our rights. All *that* suffering was *wrong* in every detail. *He* received "the due reward of *our* deeds"—He who had "done nothing amiss." That this impression may be even more upon our memories should be our constant prayer. For though we cannot expect our human frailties to cease altogether in this world, yet "God is able to make all grace abound towards us," so that even though it is required that "I know how to be abased," "I can do *all things* through Christ that strengtheneth me."

Unhappily there cannot always be reconciliation when there is forgiveness. God does not impute the trespasses of the impenitent during the day of grace. He intreats them to be reconciled. But all are not reconciled. And the same rule applies to ourselves. We may cease to impute the trespass, for Christ's sake. And we can ask reconciliation. But we cannot always insure what we ask. Offences can be forgiven at the throne of grace, and for the sake of Him that was crucified. But it is not always possible to heal the divisions that have been made in this world, or to re-unite those that have been parted by sin. Of one thing we can be sure. Where God has forgiven and man has forgiven, parting cannot be eternal. The day will come when our Saviour's prayer shall be answered—"that they all may be one."

Lead us not into Temptation.

—o—

THE way in which this petition is connected with the one that follows, shows that they are to be taken together, "Lead us not into temptation, *but* deliver us from evil."

The first of the two petitions contains an allusion to the Tempter, Satan; the second refers to the Deliverer, or Redeemer, the Lord Jesus Christ. We pray that we may *not* be brought into the power of the Tempter, that we *may* be handed over to the Deliverer, who came to "destroy the works of the devil." These two petitions also recognise the existence of the two natures in every Christian man; the flesh which lusteth against the Spirit, and the Spirit that lusts against the flesh. The one is the source of our danger in the hour of temptation. The other is the only part of us that shall be delivered from evil at the last. There is no deliverance from evil for that corrupt nature which "is not subject to the law of God, neither indeed can be." It is not sanctified, nor can it be glorified. It is to be crucified, nailed to the Cross of Christ, mortified and subdued here, and put off for ever "when our change shall come."

It is the presence of this corrupt nature in us that makes the necessity to pray, "Lead us not into temptation." And when we do fall into temptation, and give way to it, this it is that makes the Christian cry out for deliverance: "O wretched man that I am, who *shall deliver me* from the body of this death? I thank God through Jesus Christ our Lord."

Some thought is necessary in order to perceive how much the prayer, "Lead us not into temptation," really means. We cannot hope that any prayer of ours will take us absolutely clear of all temptation for a single day or a single hour. For that we "must needs go out of the world;" and as our Saviour did not ask this for those whom He loved,—though He might have asked anything,—we cannot suppose that He taught them to ask it for themselves. "I pray *not* that Thou shouldest take them *out of the world*, but that Thou shouldest keep them from the evil." Somewhere between these two boundaries, between the being taken out of the world entirely, which Christ did not pray for, and being kept out of the evil in the world, which He did, will be the land of temptation, the region of the prayer, and the possibilities both of danger and safety that it suggests. There are some things of which we can say at once that this petition is directed against them. It is written of our Saviour that He was "led up of the Spirit into the wilderness *to be tempted* of the devil;" that "He was there in the wilderness forty days;" that the closing scenes of that temptation consisted of three terrible assaults of different kinds, each of them most subtle, most trying, most perilous. And not until "the devil had ended every temptation," did he withdraw from the Holy One, and then only "for a season." We know that he came again at the hour appointed for "the power of darkness." And the prayers and supplications, and the agony in the Garden of Gethsemane, bear witness to us how terrible were Satan's last assaults.

The "twelve legions of angels" which Christ then mentioned, though He did not ask for them, suggest that He was conscious of the presence of other legions, that were *not* angels of light. At that time Christ specially instructed His disciples to remember this prayer, "Pray that ye enter not into temptation," and "Watch and *pray*, that ye enter not into temptation; the spirit indeed is willing, but the flesh is weak." Against such temptations as were brought to bear upon our Saviour in the wilderness at the beginning of His public ministry, and on the night of His betrayal at the end, we may most surely pray, "Lead us not into temptation." In this one particular we are taught to ask God unconditionally *not* to expose our weakness to Satanic strength, but to "*deliver* us from evil." This brings us to consider the possibilities of temptation for each of us in different degrees, and what it may be that can determine the question whether a Christian man shall be sorely tempted or not.

There is indeed nothing more remarkable in the petition before us than this. We are to *pray*, "Lead us not into temptation." Then, we ask, is it an open question whether we shall be tempted or not? Can we hope to escape temptation by much prayer against it? And on what does the answer to this prayer depend? We are much in the dark upon this matter. We know nothing but what God has revealed to us in His Word. Our own individual experience is, I suspect, very uniform in the matter of temptation. As far as our fallen nature is concerned, there does not seem much reason to expect that our powers of resistance will increase. We can understand what it is to escape temptation by a way that God leaves open. But to enter into it, to be pressed up to our full strength and to come out victorious without failure! Is this kind of experience common? or is it, on the contrary, extremely rare? I believe that we are saved from certain sins to which human nature is prone, and our own individual nature especially so, more by the fact that God preserves us from meeting with temptation where the opportunity for evil is very great, the chances of rebuke and observation very small, and right influences for the moment out of the way—than by any power of resistance that we possess.[1] I cannot tell to what conclusions the experience of others may bring them, but it seems to me, that with every day a belief in the weakness of our mortal nature must reasonably increase, and a belief in its strength under any trial that thoroughly tests it must diminish more and more. For myself I have every confidence that in strong temptation I should give way, and no confidence at all that I should be able to stand. That God should not lead us into any such fearful conflicts with Satan as our Saviour had to endure, seems to

[1] Compare 1 Sam. xxv. 33, 34, 39.

me an absolute necessity if we are to escape grievous sin.

We know that the new man "cannot sin, because he is born of God." We know that we "can do all things through Christ that strengtheneth us." But even the best of us are at present such mixtures of the old and the new nature, that any great pressure of temptation to evil is a very serious thing to undergo. And what necessity is there that man should be led into temptation, such temptation as this prayer asks God to remove? What necessity was there for Christ to be tempted in the wilderness? Is there any similar necessity for us to be so tempted now? The necessity that Christ our Saviour should be tempted with the utmost possible strength of temptation, is clear. Man's soul was committed to his own keeping, and the world was given to man, when God made him at the first. Man sold himself, and the world with him, to Satan; and if Satan was not to keep it for ever, man must take it out of his hands. When God became man and undertook the work of deliverance, it was necessary that He should fight the battle with Satan, and fight it out alone. It was *that* conflict that took the will of man out of Satan's power.

The Lord Jesus Christ and Satan stood face to face, will against will, in the forty days of temptation. And Jesus Christ had His own will, and kept His own way—the way of obedience to the will of His Father—to the very last. In Him human nature regained its freedom, chose the way of God, and kept it. And from that time, if Christ be in the heart of any man, the devil cannot compel that man to do wrong. That is, he cannot compel the Christ that is formed in him to sin; or turn that will one hair's breadth aside from the will of God. Whatever may be the prominent thing in the life of Christ as *we* look at it, the thing engraven on *His* memory was temptation through it all. No memory but One retains the experience of all that He endured. It was not given to the Evangelists to record what more pleasant ways He might have taken, the other words He might have spoken, the other works He might have preferred had He listened to the tempter's voice. The gospel tells us a little—not of what He avoided, but of what He did. The course that He actually took is mapped out before us. The countless by-paths that were open before Him are not set down. The outline of His life is given. Who can fill up the outline of that which is, with the possibilities of that which might have been? It is out of the question. But He who summed up His public life in the words "My temptations" knew what a reality it all was. And we have to thank Him for that reality, though we know it not. For the unknown temptations of our Saviour are ours as well as all that are written. His unknown victories are ours. By all that unwritten experience we know that "He was in all points tempted like as we are, yet without sin."

We can see that if Christ had not been tried to the uttermost, our deliverance from evil would not have been complete.

But it is complete now. And no further temptations are necessary to perfect the deliverance of human nature from the devil, or to make the victory of the Second Man over Satan more decisive than it is. The nature of Christ is as the fine gold purified in the furnace; the utmost heat of the fire has been kindled upon it, and it has come forth fine gold. No second exposure is necessary. No renewal of the heat of the furnace will make the gold finer than it is now. There was no dross in Him at any time. "The prince of this world cometh," He said, "and hath *nothing* in ME."

And if there was no dross then, there is none now. So there is no necessity to tempt Christians as Christ was tempted in order to prove the perfection of the nature of Christ. The only thing necessary to prove was, that He could really dwell in His disciples and exhibit the strength of His own holiness in their lives. That fact was soon proved to satisfaction in the history of the early Church. Satan must soon have been well aware that he had no more power against the Christ in a disciple than he had against the Christ Himself. Something of the same kind must take place in every Christian. His faith must be tried or proved to show that it is there and to give him experience of the strength of God and of His grace. The man who thus *endures* temptation shall receive "the crown of life." There is a beautiful allusion in the Prophet Zechariah (chap. vi. 14 *sq.*) to this endurance and this victory. The allusion is disguised in our English Bible because it arises out of the meaning of an Old Testament name. We read it thus, "The crowns shall be to Helem, and to Tobijah and to Jedaiah, and to Hen the son of Zephaniah, for a memorial in the temple of the LORD." These Hebrew names, like all the names in the same language, have a meaning. And the ancient translation of the Scriptures, which was commonly read in the early Christian congregations, and in the synagogues of the dispersed Jews, translated the names thus, with reference to the true Jerusalem which is the Church of God: "The crown shall be to those that *endure* in her, and to them that are profitable to her, and to them that have acknowledged her, and for grace of the son of Zephaniah, and for a Psalm in the house of the Lord." There are many crowns to be given and many lovers of Jerusalem to be crowned, but first of all among them come those in her that *endure.*

Temptation for God's people may also be necessary for the sake of other beings who see our conflict but are unseen by us. It is certain that "the Lord knoweth them that are His," and when He has given His Holy Spirit to any one, He has no need to try them in order to find out if the Holy Spirit is there. But there is another reason which sometimes makes it necessary for us to be tempted besides this. The reason lies with ourselves. If *we* do not know the weakness or wickedness of our own natural hearts (and it is necessary that we should know it, to bring down our pride, and teach us that "in our flesh dwelleth no good thing"), then we may be led into temptation, that we may know how frail we are. Thus it is written that Hezekiah was tempted (2 Chron. xxxii. 31). "God left him to try him, to know all that was in his heart." Not that God drew him into sin, but He allowed one who thought himself strong enough to stand, to try whether he could walk alone. If the humble are tried, they will probably be faithful like Abraham; but "*pride* goeth before destruction, and a haughty spirit before a fall." Pride, and whatever feeds pride, are the things most likely to spoil the effect of this prayer. There is a passage in the First Epistle to Timothy which illustrates this. Speaking of our position in this world, St. Paul says, "We brought nothing into this world, and it is certain we can carry nothing out . . . but they that *will be rich*, fall into temptation and a snare." He does not say they that *are* rich. A person may be born rich, or wealth may come to them unsought. But they who persist in seeking it, who *choose* and *prefer* to be rich, fall into temptation, because their means help to support their pride. We conclude then that this part of our Lord's prayer belongs especially to a humble spirit, dwelling in the fear of God.

Those who know their own strong propensities to evil, and desire to escape, may find comfort in praying, "Lead us not into temptation," in the confidence that the prayer itself is security for an answer. Those who have besetting sins to contend with, and find the conflict an unequal one, may consider whether they have made the most of the petition given them in these words.

They may pray that God would not bring them into any position where their besetting temptations is likely to press them hard. There is no cowardice in this. I believe it to be that true discretion which is the better part of valour. It may be very manly to resolve to meet the enemy and stand and win the victory. But what is the use of preaching manliness to a slave? "I am carnal, *sold* under sin; I know that in me, that is in my flesh, dwelleth no good thing." Surely I need not run into temptation only to discover what I may know already if I will, that I cannot stand against it. One "lead us not into temptation" is better than many vows and resolutions to sin no more. "We wrestle not against flesh and blood," but against a foe that no fallen child of Adam ever overcame. Of him, far more than of any other creature, the words of the Lord are true. "The sword of him that layeth at him cannot hold; the spear, the dart, nor the breast-plate. He esteemeth iron (our iron will) as straw, and brass (all our brightness and courage) as rotten wood. The arrow cannot make him flee; sling-stones are turned with him into stubble; darts are counted as stubble, He laugheth at the shaking of a spear. Upon earth there is not his like, who is made without fear." And if I may be allowed to borrow some other words of the same passage of Scripture, the warning of the Lord of hosts to all His soldiers is this: "Lay thine hand upon him; remember the battle, do no more." Is there not teaching for us in these words? We must indeed lay our hand upon him, but not presume to meet him with our own weapons at all. Only "remember the battle," the battle in Eden, the battle in the wilderness, and the battle which you yourself have fought, and fought in vain. Remember the battle in Eden, and how the purest unaided humanity failed, and always must fail, to stand. Remember the battle in the wilderness, and how Satan failed as utterly as Adam failed before. Stay yourself upon that battle; and "*do no more.*" "Come near and put your feet upon the necks of these kings." Lay your hand upon your adversary; but do not forge any weapon or attempt to strike him yourself. Call upon Christ to stand up and fight for you, to take the battle upon Himself, and not lead you into temptation. And if we ask in faith, our Father in heaven will answer this prayer in ways that we know not. Our sinful thoughts and desires would not be so continually pressing us if we prayed more beforehand that they might not come. If we cannot go out of the world, let us reduce to the smallest amount possible the chances that bring us into danger from the evil that is in the world. Our Saviour "knew what was in man" when he bade us decline the conflict when we can. We shall do well to take His advice. Remember how he said to the foremost of His apostles, "Simon, Simon, behold, Satan hath desired to have you that he may sift you as wheat; but I have prayed for thee that thy faith fail not." Christ gave Himself to prayer in prospect of temptation. If we would escape from falling, we must do likewise. Angels "kept not their first estate," but fell in time of temptation. There is only one hand that is able to keep us from falling,—our *Father's* hand. He gives us to our Saviour and the Saviour has committed us to Him. "My sheep hear My voice, and I know them, and they follow Me. And I give unto them eternal life; and they shall never perish, neither shall any man pluck them out of my hand. My Father who gave them Me is greater than all, and no one is able to pluck them out of my Father's hand."

Deliver us from Evil.

—o—

THE points in this last petition of the Lord's Prayer are few and simple, though they include a great deal. The word "deliver" introduces the work and office of the Lord Jesus into the prayer. We begin with "our Father," we end with our "Deliverer," His Son Jesus Christ. A quotation from the prophet Isaiah in Rom. xi. enables us to trace this word "deliverer" to its home in Old Testament prophecies and types. "There shall come out of Zion *the Deliverer*," we read in Rom. xi. 26, where the word for "Deliverer" is akin to the "deliver" of the Lord's Prayer. In Isa. lix. 20 we read, "The *Redeemer* shall come to Zion." The Redeemer in Israel had special duties. He was the "near kinsman," and the "avenger" or "redeemer" of blood. The law of Moses laid the brother or nearest male relative under obligation to buy his brother back from slavery, to avenge him if he died by violence, and to raise up the name of the dead on his inheritance if he died and left no seed. All these obligations were undertaken by the Lord Jesus when He became "partaker of flesh and blood." He then became our Redeemer, our near kinsman. To buy us back from slavery, to redeem our soul from the hand of hell, to raise up the dead to inherit the land of promise, all these duties devolved upon our Saviour "when for us men and for our salvation" He was made *man.* He revealed Himself as a redeemer to Israel from the very first. As "the angel that redeemed me from all evil," He was known to Jacob. He revealed Himself to Israel in Egypt under the same obligation, I am Jehovah, and *I will redeem.*

And when we say "*Deliver* us from evil" in the Lord's Prayer, we appeal to the Redeemer and to the whole of His redeeming work. "Doubtless Thou art our Father, our Redeemer." We ask to be numbered with those "whom the Lord hath redeemed and delivered from the hand of the enemy."

"Deliver us from evil," and "redeem us from the wicked one," are both equally correct versions of the petition. In the prayer "Lead us not into temptation," we hint at the danger which we incur from the tempter. In this last petition we speak of the wicked one by name. Not that the one meaning of the prayer need exclude the other. It is no doubt intended that the expression here used should have *two* meanings, "*evil,*" and "the *evil one*"—the thing, and the person who wields the power of it. Without the person the thing itself would scarcely exist. It was the evil one who first tempted our parents to seek the knowledge of evil. "Ye shall be as gods, knowing good and evil." The knowledge of good was present already. Evil was the only additional element which remained to be known. We who transgressed, that we might "know good *and evil,*" now pray to be delivered from the evil that we have so long known.

In the evil here described we include Satan and all the system in which he moves; the wickedness of the wicked one in all its influence and in all its effects. There is no reason to doubt that human suffering and misery are to a very large extent, if not altogether, the work of him who has the power of death, the devil. We read in Scripture of the "evil day," that is, the day when we need to stand up against Satan "in the whole armour of God." His angels are "evil spirits." The oppression and unkindness which move men to strife are his wickedness. His servants are an "evil generation," and all his deeds in general are "*deeds of darkness.*" We ourselves acknowledge this in a very curious way. Whenever any great calamity occurs, what pains and time we spend to *throw light upon it.* How we ransack everything that can possibly give us a clue to the cause of the mischief done. And how often the calamities that befall us remain "*deeds of darkness*" to the last. Preventible in so many ways, but not prevented, and not to be accounted for in the way they actually occurred. In this kind of evil or wickedness, we are told that the whole world lieth, and there it must lie, until "the kingdoms of this world shall become the kingdoms of our Lord and of His Christ," and this present evil world shall be no more. From "this *present* evil world" Christ died that He might deliver us, even while it is present, and before it shall pass away. And our gradual deliverance from evil is the whole progress of our union with Him. To be in Christ is to be delivered. To have Christ is to have the deliverer and the deliverance in ourselves. In this petition we ask one thing and one only, to be made perpetual "partakers of Christ."

The word "evil" in the Lord's Prayer has been the subject of much discussion since the appearance of the Revised Version of the English New Testament." "Deliver us from the Evil One" is the translation which the Revisers have preferred. They would have materially strengthened their position if they had translated the sentence thus, "Deliver us from the *wicked* one." The fact that the word "evil" really means "wicked," is the strongest reason for supposing that there is a reference to Satan here. For, strictly speaking, only *persons* can be wicked. There is no *wickedness* in *things* without life. If we find them *troublesome*, it is because we lack the knowledge or the power which is necessary in order to deal with them. The forces of nature, or the workings of disease, often seem to baffle the skill of man with a kind of deliberate malice, as though they had set themselves to thwart him on purpose. This resistance, however, has no "wickedness" about it, speaking strictly, unless we suppose that the wicked one lies behind it, concealing himself in the apparent workings of the material world. Now the word for *evil* in the Lord's Prayer is very rarely applied, either in the Old or New Testament, to things that are not wicked. "A noisome and grievous (*i.e. wicked*) sore fell on the men that had the mark of the beast" (Rev. xvi.) "A corrupt tree bringeth forth evil (*i.e. wicked*) fruit" (St. Mark vii. 17, 18). These are the only two examples in the New Testament where the word is used of things that have no *moral* qualities. And in the Greek Version of the Old Testament, the instances where the word is used of things incapable of voluntary action are, comparatively, very few.

A very interesting question arises out of these facts concerning the meaning of "evil" in Holy Scripture. If it were not for moral evil, *wickedness*, would there be any material evil in the world? And it would seem that there would not. For the forces of nature never do us any harm which knowledge could not prevent, and which proper care, if we had the necessary knowledge, would not enable us to avoid. Short of the absolute destruction of this habitable globe, there is no natural convulsion which man might not survive if he knew the proper means to employ for self-protection. And loss of property might be avoided if we knew what would occur. For we cannot suppose for one moment that the Creator would ever leave all His creatures to perish by any natural convulsion, unless man had incurred His anger by opposition to His will. Calamities arising from man's wickedness and ignorance are all traceable to sin. Something of this kind seems to be intended by the saying in Proverbs, "When a man's ways please the Lord, He maketh even his enemies to be at peace with him." Eliphaz the Temanite seems to have had the same thought concerning those who are under divine protection when he said, "At destruction and famine thou shalt laugh; neither shalt thou be afraid of the beasts of the earth. For *thou shalt be in league with the stones of the field,* and the beasts of the field shall be at peace with thee" (Job v. 22, 23). Even in this present evil world we learn that "*all things work together for good* to them that love God."

And to return to the words of the Lord's Prayer. "Deliver us from evil" clearly means, in the first place, deliver us from *the* evil, *i.e.*, the supreme evil of disobedience to the will of our Heavenly Father, and from his power who is pre-eminently *the evil one,* the wicked one, "the spirit that worketh in the children of disobedience." It is only his action that makes evil among the works of God. All that God has made and set to work is *very good.* Those who receive hurt in the midst of His work are like careless persons among sound machinery. They may lose their lives or receive severe injury, but it is not the machinery that is in fault; it is their own heedlessness and infirmity. And this is moral evil. Remove this, and all other evil departs with it. Hence we may safely say that there is no mention of physical apart from moral evil in the Lord's Prayer. It goes on the same principle as "Seek ye first the kingdom of God and His righteousness, and all these things shall be added unto you." Seek deliverance from the wicked one, and you shall escape all evil. Its power to harm you shall cease. In this spirit it was said, by one whose life was one long illustration of the truth, that it is the privilege of the believer to rise superior to all circumstances.

Men of the world are turned hither and thither by them. To the Christian it is said, "All things are yours, whether things present, or things to come—*all are yours*." We may not always have the grace to see it. And it is not meant that our prayers will always avail to remove sorrow or pain or distress of "mind, body, or estate." But we may always have grace to use things present for God's glory, and we may always commit things present to God in prayer. If we desire that they should be altered, why not ask it? "Who can tell if God will be gracious to us" in the very way which we desire? And if not in that way, He will assuredly "deliver us from the evil," and make all work together for good.

Many examples and illustrations of this prayer may be found in holy Scripture. The prayer and experience of Jabez has much in common with the language of this petition. Let us take it as an example of what is meant by deliverance from evil in this present evil world.

"And Jabez called on the God of Israel, saying, Oh that Thou wouldest bless me indeed, and enlarge my coast, and that Thine hand might be with me, and that Thou wouldest keep me from evil that it may not grieve me" (1 Chron. iv. 10).

This means literally "Do from evil," that is, Deal not ill (with me), but work in a contrary direction, that it (evil) may not grieve me. Somewhat in the same sense we pray, "O Lord, deal not with us after our sins, neither reward us according to our iniquities."

H

We may well believe that Jabez referred to the evil that lay within him, if we notice the word *grieve* in his prayer. What does he mean by "grieve?" The word he used enables us to answer this question. He alluded to his own name of Jabez given him by his mother (see verse 9). His mother called him "Jabez, sorrowful" (he causeth grief), saying, "because I bare him with sorrow." Against the fulfilment of his own name in the circumstances of his life Jabez prayed to the God of Israel, "Behold, to trouble I was begotten, and in sorrow did my mother bear me; but work Thou for the removal of this evil, that it may not grieve me: that my name, 'he causeth grief,' be not fulfilled in myself and in those about me, but that though I am sorrowful my sorrow may be turned into joy."

The prayer becomes applicable to all of us when we see that this grief and sorrow are the very things entailed upon us by the curse in the day of the Fall, the very things from which Christ hath redeemed us, "being made a curse" on our behalf. "The Lord God said unto the woman, I will greatly multiply thy *sorrow* and thy conception: in *sorrow* thou shalt bring forth children." The *sorrow* of Jabez' mother was a literal fulfilment of this very thing. But it is not woman's portion only. It was said to Adam besides, "Cursed is the ground for thy sake: in *sorrow* shalt thou eat of it all the days of thy life." This sorrow is Jabez and the inheritance of Jabez, and of all of us by natural descent. Whatever be our inheritance in God's land of promise, this tendency to grief we inherit from our father Adam, without any will and testament, by the law of our being. And unless the God of Israel had enlarged our coast, in this inheritance we had been shut up with sorrow for evermore. But if any man be in Christ, there is a new nature implanted within for this life present. And for the life to come, there is the promise that "there shall be no more death, neither *sorrow* nor crying, neither shall there be any more pain, for the former things shall have passed away."

"That Thou wouldest keep me from evil that it may not grieve me." This prayer in its fulness involves the whole of redemption, the whole work of the Saviour and the Holy Spirit in the soul of man. Christ "gave Himself for our sins that He might deliver us from this present evil world." He has given the Holy Spirit that He may renew us and "sanctify us wholly,—that our whole spirit and soul and body may be preserved, to be blameless at His coming." He does not forget the existence of evil around us and within us. He does not ask us to forget it in our prayers, or to speak as if there was no such thing. Rather by this example he encourages us to pray, that though the evil is here, it may not work its consequences upon us; that the curse, which is the whole sum of evil in this present evil world, may never wholly fall upon our heads; that for His sake who was made a curse for us we may not come to everlasting grief.

The prayer of Jabez in this part agrees with Psalm cxxxix.: "Search me, O God, and know my heart, try me and know my thoughts; and look well if there be any way of pain or grief in me," anything that will lead me to the grief that comes of evil if it remains unchecked at the last. "Look well if there be any way of grief in me, and lead me in the way everlasting."

But there remains another form of "evil" besides those of which we have spoken. We have acknowledged our guilt and prayed for forgiveness. We have asked to be delivered from the power of sin, and to be kept from temptation. We have prayed against this present evil world and its attractions. But still the consequences of former sin remain to be considered, even when for Christ's sake the Lord hath put away its penalty. How many "matters of iniquity prevail against us" beside the actual sin! To many of us these seem the most trying part of our case. Matters connected with our sin "prevail against us" like the waters of the Deluge over the earth, like a giant in the day of battle. It is not forgiveness only that we need. There may still remain consequences in this life present, consequences which for our part we cannot avoid. We say to ourselves, that though the sin may be forgiven it is impossible to undo the past. Thus do "matters of iniquity *prevail* against us." But even here we are encouraged to believe that God can "deliver us from evil." For the Psalmist goes on with his confession in these words, "As for our transgressions, Thou shalt purge them away." He does not say our unrighteousness, or sin, merely, but our *transgressions*, our actual falls and mistakes and trespasses, the very things that we expect to make our life bitter, that have perhaps embittered it in great part already—such transgression and disobedience as often in this life "receive a just recompense of reward."

"Thou, O God, that hearest prayer, Thou shalt purge them away!" And when He says "purge them" He means cover them, make reconciliation for them, bring mercy to bear upon them, heal the sores and close the breaches that have been made by them. All these things he says without hesitation that God will do. "As for our transgressions"—I do not say only Thou *canst*, but—Thou *shalt*, Thou dost purge them away.

When Christ has thus delivered us from the guilt and the power and the consequences of sin, it remains only that He should finish the work of Redemption in its full and final sense by delivering us from this present evil world. This He has done in part for many individual disciples by receiving them unto Himself. This He will accomplish fully for *all* His disciples when He comes again. This it is that the children of God wait for "the Redemption (the deliverance) of our body." When we think of that deliverance we may well go on to mention "the kingdom, and the power, and the glory" that will remain when the children of God shall not "see evil any more." And thus we may conclude with St. Paul, "The Lord shall deliver me from every evil work, and will preserve me unto His heavenly kingdom, to whom be glory for ever and ever. Amen."

"For thine is the Kingdom, the Power, and the Glory, for ever. Amen."

[NOTE.—Our Revisers have omitted the doxology from the text of the New Testament, and transferred it to the margin. Some of the highest textual authorities consider that they erred in so doing. But for English readers it seems sufficient to propound the following view of the matter. The doxology is connected with the prayer by the important word FOR, *i.e.*, BECAUSE. We ask Thee, O Father, for all these things, *Because Thine is the kingdom, the power, and the glory, for ever.* Now seeing that this doxology is found in versions of the New Testament much older than the most ancient MSS. which omit it, and that the Greek fathers from Chrysostom downwards accepted it, and expounded it in relation to the preceding petitions, it seems quite fair to put this question, Which is more likely, that some copies of the Gospel should have wrongly omitted this sentence, as they have wrongly omitted many others, or that any early writer should have presumed *to add to our Lord's own words the reasons for this pattern prayer?* If any form of words was ever held sacred, certainly this must have been. "Ye shall not add unto the word which I command you, neither shall ye diminish ought from it," is surely applicable to the Lord's Prayer.

I cannot think that the Church of the first three centuries would have accepted any human addition to this sacred form of words. Even an Apostle would not have presumed to make it. And if not an Apostle, then who else? I believe the doxology to be a genuine portion of the original prayer.

The coincidence between the words of the doxology, as connected with the preceding clause of the prayer, and St. Paul's saying in 2 Timothy iv. 17, 18, has been pointed out more than once, and is well worthy of observation.

Deliver us *from evil*, for *thine* is the *kingdom*, the power and *the glory for ever. Amen.*—St. Matt. vi. 12, 13.	And the Lord shall *deliver* me *from* every *evil* work, and shall preserve me unto *His* heavenly *Kingdom*, to whom be *the glory for ever* and ever. *Amen.*—2 Tim. iv. 28.

We may therefore safely proceed to examine the meaning of the doxology in relation to the entire prayer. We shall find that no human intellect devised the connection. "Who hath known the mind of the Lord, or who hath been His counsellor?"]

THIS is a doxology to the whole prayer, but it is more immediately *connected with the last petition.* Deliver us from that kingdom and that power which is opposed to Thy glory, *for Thine* is all that bears the name of kingdom or power within the universe, as Thine alone is all its glory,—"Heaven and earth are full of Thy glory."

In this connection, the doxology to the Lord's Prayer suggests our Lord's answer to the third temptation. The tempter showed Him all the *kingdoms* of the world and the *glory* of them. All this *authority* will I give Thee . . . if Thou wilt fall down and worship me. But "thou shalt worship the Lord thy God, and Him only shalt thou serve." Why? For *Thine is* the *kingdom* and the power *and the glory*, world without end. When it is all Thine, why should we do homage to another for any part of it? And hence we see the connection between *the doxology and the entire prayer.* We worship Thee and Thee only, because no other has anything to give, except what is Thine. Whatever man can give, Thou hast first given to him. What principalities and powers may bestow, is bestowed upon them by Thee, to whom it belongs both to give and to take away, —blessed be Thy name. This doxology also suggests what is too often forgotten, that *the Lord's prayer is an answered prayer.* To Him who made it the Lord has said, "Sit Thou on My right hand until I make Thine enemies Thy footstool." He has glorified His name in Him. He has given Him dominion and glory and a kingdom. He has done His will in Him. From the need to ask daily bread, forgiveness, or deliverance, He has released Him for ever. And the kingdom and power and glory are *all* His. He has "set Him at His own right hand in the heavenly places, far above all principality, and power, and might, and dominion, and every name that is named, not only in this world, but also in that which is to come, and hath put all things under His feet, and *given Him to be Head over all things to the Church, which is His body*, the fulness of Him that filleth all in all."

And this brings out the Christian's security for an answer to his own petitions when he prays his

Master's prayer. "Thine is the kingdom, and the power, and the glory," and Thou hast given it all to Him, whom Thou hast not spared for my sake, but hast delivered Him up for us all. How shalt Thou not, "with Him, also freely give us all things?" It is all Thine; but Thou hast begotten a Son, and to Him Thou hast given all that Thou hast. And Thou hast given Him to us, and us to Him, and therefore we pray to Thee for the completion of that gift in all its unspeakable results to ourselves, "Hallowed be Thy name, Thy kingdom come, Thy will be done on earth, as it is in heaven, for Thine is the kingdom, the power, and the glory, for ever. Amen."

We may also trace in the doxology an acknowledgment of the three Persons of the glorious Godhead. As the prayer for the spread of God's glory and its manifestation is threefold, "Hallowed be Thy name, Thy kingdom come, Thy will be done," so the acknowledgment of His power to grant the prayer is also threefold. "For Thine is the kingdom, the power, and the glory." And we shall not err, if we seek to recognise the Persons of the Father and of the Son and of the Holy Ghost in the "kingdom" and "power" and "glory" of this doxology. For "Thine, O Father, is the kingdom." If it were not His, how could He have given it to His Son? We shall find too, that the very first conception of a kingdom originates with God. It precedes the revelation of His Son from heaven. It comes to earth and is established by the Son, that He may "deliver it up to God, even His Father," when He shall have "put down all" other "rule and authority and power."

And as the kingdom belongs to the Father, so do we ascribe the power, *i.e.*, *the ability*, to the Son. He is "the Power of God and the wisdom of God." God created all things *by Jesus Christ.* "Without *Him* was not anything made, that has been made." To Him more especially belong those manifestations of ability which make the Gospel to be "*the power of God* unto salvation to every one that believeth." Of Him it is written "that He is *able to save to the uttermost* all that come unto God by Him." Some of the loveliest passages of the New Testament are those in which this *ability* is put forth and presented to our view.

And as the kingdom of the Father is established on earth, through the manifestation of His ability in His Son, so the glory that crowns and rests upon the whole is the glory of the Holy Spirit. God is "glorious in *Holiness*." The divine beauty springs from the divine character. A kingdom and power may exhibit much that is not beautiful. It is only a *character* * for righteousness and beneficence that

* We may distinguish the difference between "authority," "ability," and "glory" in this way—

Authority without ability is contemptible.

Ability without authority is impotent or lawless.

Ability without "glory" is featureless or odious.

Take away the character, and the significance of all action is gone. Why *thus*, and not *thus*?

If there is no standard of action, why exercise control?

If no need of control, why manifest power?

I may do it.	Can I?
I can do it.	Must I?
I must do it.	Shall I?

The last and the first join. The glory of God requires Him to act, can give true glory. And God's glory is of the very essence of His Being. It is "the beauty of Holiness," the essential attribute of the Divine Spirit.

We are taught to say to our Father, "*Thine is* the kingdom, the power, and the glory, for ever." Not only "it will be," or "it may be," or "may it be," but "*Thine is* all this for ever." Thine as our Father! and therefore ours as Thy sons. It is Thine before it comes to us; it is Thine when it is manifested. And when Thou hast given it to us, it will still be Thine for ever. And we shall be Thine also, wholly Thine; "not our own, but bought with a price." Not "sold under sin," or oppressed of Satan, but Thine in "the liberty wherewith Christ hath made us free"—the sons of God, and more "after His likeness for ever." To this we say "Amen," so be it! It is so in the possibilities of Divine grace. May it be so in the accomplished work of our salvation, to the Divine glory. It is so now, when much is in force that seems opposed to it. "Thine is the kingdom," even while Satan reigns. How much more when he is cast out, and "the Lord alone shall be exalted!"

What fulness there is in this doxology when treated as the foundation of the entire prayer!

and prescribes the law of His action, "*For mine own sake*, even for Mine own sake will I do it;" "For how should my NAME be polluted?"

Thine is the Kingdom.

—o—

THIS sentence is found in the Old Testament, in a connection that is somewhat remarkable. In Chron. xxix. 11, we read, "Thine, O Lord, is the greatness, and the power, and the glory, and the victory, and the majesty; for all that is in the heaven and the earth is Thine; *Thine is the kingdom,* O Lord, and Thou art exalted as Head above all." The words were those of David, and the occasion on which they were spoken is worthy of notice. "On that day, *they made* Solomon, the son of David, king *the second time.*" And "he sat *on the throne of the Lord* as king instead of David his father" (v. 22, 23). The only temporal kingdom with which the name of God was ever directly identified was just reaching the height of its glory. All its victories had been won; its conflicts were now over; and a son had been born to the conqueror, who was to be "a man of rest." He was just established upon the throne of his father, and the kingdom was confirmed in his hand. And he was to build the temple of the Lord. For the first time in history, God's kingdom was to have a religious and a political metropolis on earth.

The king's palace and the palace that was "not for man but for the Lord God" were to stand side by side in the same city, with only a valley between them, and a lofty arch uniting the two. The political greatness of God's chosen people at this time reached its greatest height. And though the glory was but transitory, it foreshadowed "the glory that excelleth," and that shall endure for ever, when for "the second time" the son of David shall come to His own people as their King; "having salvation" which shall no more be rejected, and a kingdom of which there shall be no end. "The kingdom shall come to the daughter of Jerusalem," and this will be one fulfilment of the petition, "Thy kingdom come." The kingdom of Solomon prefigured it, and that kingdom may well serve to remind us that "the kingdom is the Lord's." With Him it rests, to establish and reveal, or to defer it and vail its glory, until the fulness of the time is come.

The clause that follows, "Thine is the kingdom," may be literally rendered thus: "Thine is the kingdom, O Lord, and he that is exalted (or *exalteth himself*) as head over all." We may fill up this sentence in two ways. "Thine is the kingdom, O Lord, and [Thou art] He that is exalted." Or, "Thine is the kingdom, O Lord, and [Thine is] he that exalteth himself as head over all." This latter way of reading the sentence is to be preferred in my opinion, and it has the support of the Jewish commentators.

"He that exalteth himself" is also the more exact rendering. Adonijah "exalted himself," 1 Kings i. 5. Compare the words of Balaam in Num. xxiv. 7, "His king shall be higher than Agag, and His kingdom *shall exalt itself.*" In these two parallels the whole breadth of the meaning may be perceived. For Adonijah was but a pretender to royalty. And Balaam was speaking of the kingdom of Christ. We thus obtain the following interpretation of David's words, and a deeply interesting interpretation it is: "Thine is the kingdom, O Lord, and Thine is every one that exalteth himself any where to be a head." God Himself is the *fountain* of all rule and all authority and power. This very expression is used by Jewish writers in their comments upon the passage. And if "every one that exalteth himself" belongs to God, how much more may we say that *He* whom God will exalt as His chosen King is His? And this is the very language of prophecy respecting our Lord. "The kings of the earth set themselves and the rulers take counsel together against the Lord, and against *His anointed.* Yet have I set *My King* upon My Holy Hill of Zion." If all kingship is from Him, how much more will He "give strength to *His King,* and exalt the horn of *His anointed?*"

In this view, then, the first clause of the doxology covers all human history. It goes back to the dawn of creation. For God made men to be kings. "Let us make man in Our image, after Our likeness, and *let them have dominion.*" This dominion, in the Divine purpose, included "all things." Its full extent can only be discovered by an examination of the New Testament use of the Psalmist's words which are founded on the first chapter of Genesis, "Thou madest Him *to have dominion* over the works of Thy hands. *Thou hast put all things in subjection under His feet.*" All things, even to death, the "last enemy;" every name that is named in this world or in the world to come;—leaving nothing not "put under Him," He only "excepted which did put all things under Him."

This was our Creator's design for us. And the kingdoms that men establish upon earth are but proofs that man was made in His image. The special connection between royalty and Deity which this truth implies may explain some of the most striking passages in the Bible. "The heaven for height, and the earth for depth, and the heart of kings is unsearchable." "The king's heart is in the hand of the Lord, as the rivers of water; He turneth it whithersoever He will." "A king, against whom there is no rising up." The kingly faculty is one of those which the Most High keeps in special control. By this He constantly orders the affairs of men, and works out the counsel of His own will. Sacred history supplies us with constant illustrations of this, both among the kingdoms of this world, and in the records of God's chosen people. What can be more remarkable than the sudden overthrow of that scheme for keeping mankind together under one central monarchy which was frustrated in the early dawn of civilization at Babel? and yet the same place was made the capital of the first great world-empire, by a kind of special Divine license granted to Nebuchadnezzar some fifteen centuries later. But what other king ever received such striking personal proofs that "the most High ruleth in the kingdom of men, and giveth it to whomsoever He will, and setteth up over it the basest of men?" Besides the defiance of his kingly word by Daniel's three fellows, and Nebuchadnezzar's own seven years' madness, to him was revealed, in outline, the history of all universal monarchies on earth, until the kingdom of Christ should come. Thus did God set bounds to man's ambition and lust of power, as He sets the sand for the bound of the sea, prescribing beforehand the limits of all human sovereignty, to teach us that every one that exalteth himself is His servant; that He Himself is "the Blessed and only Potentate, the King of all that reign, and the Master of all that rule."

But if the weakness of the kingdoms of this world proves the truth of "Thine is the kingdom" in one way, the strength and character of the kingdom of God teaches us the same lesson in another. God's kingdom has grown up on earth, within the kingdoms of this world and without them; now taking to itself a power and glory equal to theirs, and meeting them, so to speak, on their own level, as it did under David, Solomon, and more or less under some of their successors; but more often ignoring them, or even defying them; taking its own line in the teeth of their opposition, or simply going its own way and leaving them to go theirs. We may trace this in the history of the patriarchs. When they were strangers and pilgrims, and "went from one nation to another, from one kingdom to another people, God suffered no man to do them wrong; He *reproved even kings for their sakes:* Touch not *Mine anointed*, and do My prophets no harm." A little while, and He set one of those prophets, who came into the kingdom as a slave, next to the king himself in position, and above the king in real power, "God hath made me a father to Pharaoh, and lord of all his house." The story of the Exodus brings the kingdom of God and the kingdom of man into direct conflict; and the result is, that in a few weeks "Egypt is destroyed." We have not time to pursue this subject through all its ramifications in history. Enough to say that we may find God's kingdom in almost every conceivable relation to the kingdoms of this world, and always holding its own. There is one striking fact which must not be forgotten respecting the Kingdom of God in the time of what we may call its political glory, under David and Solomon. And that is the exceedingly careful and gradual preparation which was bestowed on that kingdom and its king. Only after a most protracted struggle between the principles of faith and sight, did God permit His people to enjoy the headship of a regular succession of kings, in one continuous dynasty. The head of that dynasty, David, came to the throne after a long course of special training, through a series of events which are brimming over with spiritual and prophetic meaning at every turn. And when this kingdom came, it continued only long enough to complete the picture of things to come which it foreshadowed, and then its outward and visible glory faded like the flower of the grass. The kingdom of God once more retired into the hearts, which are its only resting-place on earth, because they "hear the word of God and keep it."

"Thine is the kingdom, O Lord," receives its clearest explanation from the life of Christ. By the light of His presence we see that the real position of the kingdoms of this world is one of opposition to Him and to His doings, if the two are forced into contact. The first page of the Gospel opens with the note of war between the "born King of the Jews" and him who then reigned in Jerusalem. What Herod did in the fury of his blind passion, Pilate was compelled to do against his own sense of justice, by the deliberate malice of the Jews. Both pronounced a death sentence on the Anointed of the Lord. The life of the King of kings on earth began and ended under a sentence of death from the supreme power in Jerusalem, although it was "the city of the great King." The remarkable way in which not only our Lord but His Forerunner held themselves aloof from all office and dignity which was open to them in Israel, that they might preach the kingdom of God, is also most instructive. The disappointment of that design which would have "come and taken Him by force to make Him a king" was the occasion of one of the loftiest miracles in our Lord's earthly life. He walked upon the waters, not only in order to rejoin the disciples, whom He had sent away to prevent their entangling Him by their open acknowledgment of His Royal Majesty, but also in order to show that "the Lord on High is mightier than the noise of many waters, yea, than the mighty waves of the sea." "The waters" upon which He walked "are peoples and multitudes, and nations and tongues." He passed over them, He slept upon them, He stilled them, but He did not reign among them, because He aspired first of all to reign within them, in that kingdom which is "righteousness, and peace, and joy, in the Holy Ghost." To the "*poor* in spirit," and the "persecuted for righteousness' sake," He assigns the kingdom of heaven, but not to those that exercise lordship and authority over their brethren. "My kingdom is not of this world. If My kingdom were of this world then would My servants fight, that I should not be delivered to the Jews, but *now is my kingdom not from hence.*" "Art thou a king, then?" "*Thou* sayest that 'I am a *King*.'" "*To this end have I been born, and for this cause have I come into the world, that I may bear witness unto the truth.*"

To be a "faithful and true witness,"—yes, a MARTYR,—the chief of martyrs before He became the King of kings;—this was our Saviour's "good confession" before Pontius Pilate of the purpose for which He came. When did God's kingdom ever assert its true principles more nobly and at greater cost? He who was the Fount of all authority submitted to a death sentence from man's authority, for the sake of the kingdom of God. Obedience is its first law. Man must learn to do the will of God. And thus His King "became obedient, unto death, even the death of the Cross."

"Thine is the kingdom, O Lord," and "Thine is He whom Thou hast now highly exalted to be Head over all." "He became obedient unto death, even the death of the Cross, wherefore God also hath highly exalted Him." And not only for His own sake. He hath given Him "to be Head over all things to the church, which is His body."

When, therefore, we say, "Thine is the kingdom," we make our acknowledgments to our Heavenly Father, for the first and greatest of all His blessings, the gift of His dear Son Jesus Christ,—His King, whom He hath set at His own right hand, "who also maketh intercession for us." He is our Adam, our Lord from heaven. He hath overcome the sharpness of death for us, and opened the kingdom of heaven to all believers. "If we endure, we shall also reign with Him." "To him that overcometh will I grant to sit with Me on My throne." For "the word of the kingdom," the "gospel of the kingdom," we give thanks also. We acknowledge that all other kingdoms so called are but faint imitations of this. If they do not belong to the "authority of darkness," from which God through Christ hath delivered us, they are but rills from the fountain of honour, which is with Him. "Thine is every one that exalteth himself." "There is no power but of God." "The powers that be are ordained of God." For His sake we obey them while we live here, awaiting the great voices in heaven which shall proclaim them "the kingdoms of our Lord and of His Christ," when He shall come to "reign for ever and ever." Then shall we say, "Thine is the kingdom" indeed. "Thine, O Lord, is the greatness and the power, and the glory and the victory, and the majesty. Unto Him that loved us and washed us from our sins in His own blood—and He made us kings and priests unto God and His Father; to Him be glory and dominion for ever and ever. Amen."

And the Power.

"POWER" in this place means *ability*. It is one of a group of New Testament words which all have the same general meaning. But this word is the widest of them all, and embraces every kind of power except *authority*. Conquering might, or "mastery;" "strength" for endurance, power in action, or "energy;" "resource" for every kind of difficulty and emergency, the force of multitudes or armed "hosts," solid firmness and "stability," and if anything else is needed for doing, helping, and suffering—this word *ability* is large enough to include the whole. "Authority" alone is a distinct idea, which belongs rather to the "kingdom" already mentioned. "I can," does not always imply "I may." But, authority being granted, ability is free. And when ability means Omnipotence, as it does here, and conveys the idea of infinite possibility, it is well worthy of a place in the ascription of honour, and praise, and thanksgiving to the Godhead, which concludes the Lord's Prayer.

And as the "kingdom" in the Lord's Prayer is, first and last, the kingdom of the Father—for the

Son reigns, only in order that, when perfect obedience has become universal, He may deliver up the kingdom to God—so the "power" of God is more especially manifested in His Only-begotten Son. "Christ the power of God," is Himself the ability which we ascribe to the Father in this place. In Him, "man's extremity" becomes "God's opportunity." The inability of our mortal nature, and, indeed, of all nature without Him, is exposed for this express purpose, that God may glorify His ability in the Person of His Son. The extreme case is when we find ourselves, like the "daughter of Abraham" bound by Satan, and "to the uttermost unable to look up." It is then that we become fit objects of His compassion, who "to the uttermost is able to save."

This is the beginning of "the power of God unto salvation" in our hearts; but it is not the end. "I thank Christ Jesus our Lord, who hath *enabled* me;" "*I can* do all things in Christ which enableth me"—becomes the experience of this present life; and for the life to come we expect a "change" which is at present indescribable, but which will only be one more manifestation of "the mighty working of His *ability* to subdue all things unto Himself."

The whole value of this "ability" to us depends upon our own consciousness of inability. Not until we have learnt to say "I cannot," are we ready to give thanks to Him who "can." In this point of view, the Christian soldier's vocabulary differs altogether from that of the soldiers of this world. The last word in their vocabulary is the word "impossible." But it is the very first word in ours. Until we have learned to spell it, we shall be turned back again and again. Not until we have learned to say "I cannot," will Christ teach us how to say "I can."

All sacred history teaches this lesson. No sooner were our first parents placed in the abode which God had prepared for them, and left free to act for themselves, than they manifested their own inability to keep His gifts. The failure of the "first Adam" was never repaired until the appearance of the "last Adam." And that "second man is the Lord from Heaven,"—"God manifest in the flesh."

If our fallen nature had been able to attain the Divine likeness and dominion which were set before our first parents as the end of their creation, would not the Incarnation of the Son of God have been needless? Does not the manifestation of ability prove the greatness of the task? And yet it seems a thing so natural, and in itself so easy for the creature to obey his Creator, and lay hold of the good that is commended to his understanding, and placed within his grasp! Who that has read the story of the Fall, has not been tempted to think at one time or other that he himself would have stood firm under that temptation, or, at least, that the Fall shows an excess of feebleness wholly unworthy of the best sons and daughters of Adam in later days? But despite the theories of anthropologists, it seems certain that the human beings described in the beginning of Genesis were immeasurably superior to us in understanding, strength, and beauty—to say nothing of their having spoken face to face with their Creator and stood in His presence without fear. There must be some secret in the way of Holiness that is not apparent, if the story of the Fall is true. A strong man does not drop down exhausted before he has taken ten steps from his door into his garden in the early morning, unless there is some cause which does not appear on the surface, or some poison in the atmosphere which we cannot see. And to come to our own experience. The power of a besetting sin on human nature, apart from Christ, is a thing wholly inexplicable. You are convinced it is wrong. Nothing is easier than to determine not to give way to it. Your will is your own. There is nothing to compel you, if you do not choose to be compelled. Why then have you not overcome it and dismissed it long ago? *You cannot*, and before you gain the victory, you will confess that you cannot; that a higher ability than man can command is necessary. Or if you are possessed of an iron will that defies every besetment, you will still find some insignificant thing that stands between you and the way of salvation. There is nothing in it. It may be put aside any day, and you can go forward in the way that leadeth to eternal life. But days pass, and the difficulty is still there. *What* it is, is of no particular consequence. You cannot repent, or you cannot believe, or you cannot come to Christ, or you cannot feel that you are saved, or you cannot pray, or something. But there is one word at the beginning of it all, and that is not "*I can*," but "*I can not!*" "Thine is the ability" is a true word after all. And it is a word that we shall have to say to the Lord Jesus, or else we cannot be saved. God taught this lesson to the patriarchs and the people, the judges, the prophets, the priests and kings of ancient time in many ways. And nearly every demonstration of *their* inability was followed by some revelation of the ability of the Word of the Lord.

"I have gotten a man from the Lord" was an assertion of ability. But that saying gave place to one that was very different, "God hath appointed me another seed *instead of Abel*, whom the man that I had gotten slew."

The "father of the faithful" was called to a state of ever-increasing inability. Not until he said, "I go childless," did he receive the distinct promise of a countless seed. Not until he and his wife had both "laughed" at the very possibility, was the promised son born. "Is anything too hard for the Lord?" was the problem that was set before him. And the same words accompanied the announcement of the great solution of all impossibilities in the incarnation of the Saviour, "for with God nothing shall be impossible." The lesson of ability and inability takes a long time to learn. Men make mistakes on both sides. Man's inability has been ascribed to the Creator by the best of His servants. "Shall the flocks and the herds be slain for them to suffice them? or shall all the fish of the sea be gathered together for them to suffice them?" was the question once asked even by God's servant Moses. "Is the Lord's hand waxed short?" was the reply.

And again, men who have seen God's mighty

works in their own favour, sometimes make the mistake of transferring His ability to themselves. So did the spies who went to view the town of Ai after the miraculous fall of Jericho. "Make not all the people to labour thither; for they are few," was their report to Joshua. And the three thousand men who attacked the town were discomfited. "*All the people* of war" (Josh. viii. 1) were to go up, and a double ambush was set, before that town was taken. Not that the Divine ability had need of them. The faithful Israelites of later days had learnt the lesson well when they said, "Lord, it is nothing with Thee to help, whether with many or with them that have no power." "There is no restraint to the Lord, to save by many, or by few."

Many means of help and salvation in the Old Testament records were strangely devised to teach men the nature of Divine ability. Two men drove back the host of the Philistines from the heights of Michmash to their own place—though the mere terror of their presence had dispersed an army. Gideon's lamps and pitchers, David's sling and stone, Jehoshaphat's sweet singers who "praised the beauty of holiness" before his army, "the feeble Jews" with their families behind the wall in the time of Nehemiah, were all made instruments of the "salvation of the Lord."

One characteristic manifestation of the Divine ability consists in the *employment of what is at hand*, however apparently insufficient, to meet the need of the hour. "What hast thou in the house?" "Thine handmaid hath not anything in the house, save a pot of oil." But that pot of oil fills every vessel that can be borrowed in the neighbourhood, pays all the debts, and provides a means of subsistence for its owner.

"How many loaves have ye? go and see." "Five, and two fishes." Yet when five thousand *men*, not to mention women and children, have satisfied their hunger, there is more remaining than there was at first. When the Spirit of the Lord came upon Samson, and he *had nothing in his hand*, he rent the "lion like a kid." Another time "he found a new jawbone of an ass, and slew a thousand men therewith." Man's inability is not mended by any amount of resources. The Divine ability attains its end with whatever instrument is at hand.

There is no more striking example of this truth in all its details, than the human life of our Lord Jesus Christ. He is the Son of David, when David's throne has been vacant for six centuries, and David's family are at Nazareth, an obscure northern village of the promised land. He comes to open the Scriptures, and to bear witness to the truth. But His only preparation is the education of a village carpenter, and the opportunities of a life of thirty years occupied in that trade.

He is not only to die for His own nation, but to "gather together into one the children of God that are scattered abroad;" yet He never set foot outside Palestine, from the day when He was carried into Egypt as a helpless infant, until He died. His disciples were not taken from the nobility, the priesthood, or the educated class. They were men whose social standing was like His own. Yet they "turned the world upside down," as the result of His training. Those who had despised them as beneath contempt were compelled to recognise them as the men who "used to be with Jesus." There is a word in the New Testament which is constantly applied to man, and is intimately associated with this truth. In our English version it is rendered "vessels." In the original languages of the Bible it has a much wider meaning, and includes every kind of implement and tool. There is no more contemptible thing on earth than that which the Old Testament calls "a vessel wherein is no pleasure." Such things may be seen in abundance in every heap of refuse in the neighbourhood of a great city. There are the remains of all the "vessels of the great house." All in their time were of some use and value. Some were "vessels unto honour, meet for the Master's use." Others were "vessels unto dishonour," whose employment was less noble than serviceable. But their present place shows their true value. In themselves they are nothing. They never were worth anything except for that which they might hold, or, that which, being themselves held in a skilful hand, they might be made to do. In the hand of God, man with all his glory of strength, and wit, and skill, is but a "vessel," a tool, an implement, with an element of responsibility. He can give his consent or withhold it, whenever God deals with him. In himself, he is worthless. Only in relation to his Creator has he any value; and that value consists less in the possibilities of his nature and being, than in the direction given to his powers. "O Lord, I know that the *way of man is not in himself.* It is *not in man that walketh to direct his steps.*" Only one man ever did it,—"the man, Christ Jesus." Of Him alone we can truly say, "This man is the great power," the whole ability, "of God."

Let us look at this doxology as it comes from the lips of our Lord Jesus Christ. We have seen how He said, "Thine is the kingdom" in His temptation. When He was offered "all the kingdoms of the world and the glory of them," if He would accept them as a gift from Satan, and do homage for them to him, He refused: "Thou shalt worship the Lord thy God, and Him only shalt thou serve." In other words, "Thine is the kingdom." I can take it from no one else but Thee.

His acknowledgment of "Thine is the ability" is even more striking. "Abba, Father, all things are *possible* with Thee. *If it be possible,* remove this cup from me. Only not my will, but Thine be done." "Thine is the ability" to remove it. "Thine" too "is the ability" to accomplish what Thou wilt without removing it. And let that will be done. Even our Lord Himself here confessed His own human *inability.* He "offered up prayers and supplications with strong crying and tears unto Him *that was able* to save Him from death and was heard in that He feared; that is, "*in respect of His dread*—the horrible dread that overwhelmed Him." He cried as a willing instrument in the Father's hand, when He was breaking for lack of strength. "And there appeared unto Him an angel from heaven strengthening Him."

The Father to whom all things were possible, supplied the power. The possibility of our salvation became a reality. He was enabled to the uttermost to save, because He cried unto Him who has the kingdom *and the power.*

The ability of creation and the ability of holiness are both beyond the grasp of our understanding. It is only when we make the attempt and find "I cannot," that we form any conception of the greatness of "I can." We must wait until our eyes are opened in another world to know the full extent of that "ability," which we acknowledge in the doxology of the Lord's Prayer.

But even now there is an indescribable comfort in the name of "Him that is able" when it is applied in the New Testament to the circumstances of our need. Do not the words of the "Magnificat" itself gain more than they lose, in real force, if we say "He that is *able* hath done to me great things, and Holy is His name?" What exquisite irony (apparent understatement of the truth) is there in such a sentence as "We have not an High Priest who *is not able* to be touched with the feeling of our infirmities, but was in all points tempted like as we are, yet without sin." "In that He Himself hath suffered, being tempted, *He is able* to succour them that are tempted." "If Thou art able to do anything, have compassion." If Thou art able! *All* things are possible (there is nothing beyond ability) to him that believeth! "Believe ye that I am able to do this?"

These passages have often been collected and exhibited together. The gospel itself is "ability of

God unto salvation" to every believer—an ability which may be manifested in every kind of working here, and of which the possibilities are beyond conception in the life to come. For when we say "thine is *the* ability" we do not limit it by our conceptions of our present need. The length and breadth and depth and height of that ability are boundless. Surely they that are "accounted worthy to attain that world," where their Master is preparing a place for them, and the resurrection which is the very masterpiece of His ability,—surely *they* shall know what their Master can do. Therefore we give thanks for the ability that is laid up in Him. We are thankful that it is not committed to us. Enough if we can guide what we have in the spirit of obedience to our Father's will. We are content even to "glory in our infirmities," if the ability of Christ may overshadow us, in the secret of His tabernacle. "When I am weak, then am I able." For He is the Almighty God. And "he that dwelleth in the secret place of the most High shall abide under the shadow of the Almighty."

And the Glory.

"THINE is the glory" is a sentence that would seem fitter for the lips of angels than for men. It is not *impossible* that the angels join their desires to ours in the first three petitions of the Lord's Prayer. They may well wish to see the Name of God hallowed, His kingdom come, His will done on earth as they see it in heaven. But it is *certain* that they can say, "Thine is the glory." "To Thee Cherubim and Seraphim continually do cry." "And one cried unto another and said, Holy, Holy, Holy, is the Lord of Hosts. The whole earth is full of His glory." Thus Isaiah overheard them, when He saw His glory who is our Saviour, and their King, "the Lord of glory." They "rest not day and night" from this outpouring of celestial praise. The New Testament form of the song suggests its eternal freshness, for they say, "Holy, Holy, Holy, Lord God Almighty, *which is, and which was, and which is to come.*" The contemplation of His present Holiness is first. "They give glory to Him which is." But they do not forget their past visions of His glory, and they anticipate fresh revelations of it from Him "which is to come."

But what is God's glory? The word glory is one which conveys false, or very indistinct notions to the natural mind. And even in Holy Scripture it does not seem always to have one simple meaning. For example, it is often associated with literal brightness and light. "The glory of the Lord came from the way of the East; and *the earth shined with His glory*." "The glory of the Lord *shone round about them*." "I could not see for the *glory of that Light*." In such passages as these the glory is a visible brightness. But when we read of some who were convinced that Jesus is the Christ, but "would not confess Him because they loved the glory of men more than the glory of God," we can see that the word means honour, reputation, esteem. And when we read that "man is the image and glory of God, but woman is the glory of man," it is evident that glory means likeness and beauty, or a beautiful likeness. When translated literally, the New Testament word for glory is "semblance." That which God *seems* to be when He reveals Himself, the appearance that He manifests to men, is His glory. When man was created he was intended to be an embodiment of divine beauty, in his form and character and action. Woman was made to be the embodiment of human beauty. In her is concentrated the beauty as distinct from the strength of the human race.

What is called beauty, and honour, and brightness in man, is called "glory" in God. Strictly the word glory is almost limited to God, and to man as His image. For "all the glory of man is as the flower of grass." "The grass withereth, the flower fadeth," but "the glory of the Lord shall endure for ever." He is "the Father of glory," Christ is "the Lord of glory." The Holy Spirit is "the Spirit of glory." And God's glory can only be known by revelation. It is fitly named at the close of the Lord's Prayer, because it is that which He manifests in man and in the world, as the result of His work in creation and redemption. His kingdom and power will show His glory. And the gospel is "the gospel of the glory of Christ" who is His image. The gospel reveals "the wisdom of God in a mystery, the hidden wisdom, which God ordained before the world *unto our glory* (*i.e.*, to bring us to glory), which none of the princes of this world knew; for, had they known it, they would not have crucified *the Lord of glory*. But, as it is written, Eye hath not seen, nor ear heard, neither have entered into the heart of man, the things which God hath prepared for them that love Him. But *God hath revealed them unto us by His Spirit;* for the Spirit searcheth all things, even the depths of God."

What, then, is God's glory? The praise of the angels connects it always with His *holiness*. He is "glorious in holiness." And His holiness is part of His very Being. For He teaches us that He is Spirit. And when we speak of Him by that name, we are taught to regard Him as a *Holy* Spirit. "Spirit is the word that describes the Divine Being. Holiness is the word that describes His character. And glory is the word that describes His likeness, when men see Him in any measure as He is. God is a glorious God, because He is a Holy Spirit. It is most necessary that we should believe this, and, so far as possible, understand it. Otherwise our ideas of "glory" will be mistaken, or defective. The word itself too often conveys no definite notion to our minds. To some, perhaps, its very vagueness makes part of its attractiveness. It has possibilities which we cannot exactly calculate, and therefore there is the more to admire. But it should never be forgotten that vagueness is the parent of error. In a fog men cannot see things as they are. The mirage in the desert is often beautiful. But it is only a cloud landscape after all. And if the glory that dazzles our eyes is only mirage, we shall "lie down in sorrow" when the sun sets and the day is done.

The word which all men understand, and which comes nearest to glory, is "beauty." "Beauty" is human glory, and glory is divine beauty. And in all true beauty there is *character*. Mere physical beauty, without character, soon ceases to please. A face with all the features perfect, all the complexion clear, and everything in due proportion, soon tires us if character is absent from its looks. It becomes displeasing, if it takes any expression which is unworthy of the person on whose countenance it rests. We all acknowledge that expression, or character, is essential to the beauty of the "human face divine." But the expression is not always easily interpreted. As we read it, it seems to be an outcome of the soul that is within. But sometimes we transfer to the face which is before us an expression or intention which answers to it in our own minds, but is not really there. In other words, we do not always read countenances correctly. Sometimes, when our reading of the countenance has given one interpretation of the expression, and our reason has contradicted it, we have lived to find that our reason was mistaken, and our reading of the countenance was true. But, since most human souls are the scene of more or less conflict, it is not easy to distinguish the expression of transitory feeling on the countenance from that which belongs to the permanent character of the life.

And if we cannot always interpret the human countenance correctly, how can we read the expression on the face of God? What mistaken notions we form to ourselves of His glory! "Thou thoughtest wickedly that I am even such an one as thyself," He says to the ungodly. "Blessed are the pure in heart, *for they shall see God*," is a certain passport to the beatific vision. Only let us remember that it is not natural purity that is meant. "*He that is washed* needeth not save to wash his feet, but *is pure*, every whit." Too often those who are loudest in the praise of purity are the last to commend the cleansing blood of Jesus Christ. But without that, "who can say I have made my heart clean, I am pure from my sin?" "There is a generation that are pure in their own eyes, and yet is not washed from their filthiness." Again, since "the whole earth is full of God's glory," there are many who profess to read the expression of His countenance in the natural world. They are so busy searching for it there, that they do not think it worth while to look for it anywhere else. And do they find it there? Does everything that can be seen in creation radiate from the glory of the Creator? Or is there another influence at work? For us who believe the Bible the question is answered easily. Although "God saw everything that He had made, and behold it was very good," He himself has pointed out the introduction of a different element. When He said, "Thorns also and thistles shall it bring forth to thee," and "Cursed is the ground for thy sake," was He still speaking of that which is "very good?" And when He says "the wolf also shall dwell with the lamb, and the leopard shall lie down with the kid; and the calf and the young lion and the fatling together; and a little child shall lead them . . . they shall *not hurt nor destroy* in all My *holy* mountain: for the earth shall be full of the knowledge of the Lord, as the waters cover the sea," does He express entire approval of the present state of things, in which so large a part of the animal creation lives by taking other lives? Is this the "beauty of holiness" which His "holy mountain" is to display? Evidently it is not. It is clear that even the harmony of nature is not yet consistent with perfect holiness. And thus, though God's glory is "the fulness of the earth," there is that on earth which is not yet brought into perfect harmony with His glory. Man cannot gaze upon the face of nature and be sure that they are contemplating only the Divine glory, unless they can distinguish the good which He Himself created to reflect His image, from the mischief which disobedience has introduced. Evil habits in man are laws of nature. There is nothing more unalterable. May there not be evil habits in the natural world? We think there may. And we take leave to ascribe these to the author of evil. We refuse to read them as lines of beauty in the true face of nature which God gave her at the first. But we, alas, are tainted with evil in our own sight and judgment. We turn sadly from the contemplation of nature, and confess that there we cannot say of *all that we see*, "Thine is the glory." All the glory of the natural world is Thine, indeed. Thy glory is the fulness of the earth. It is "empty and void, and waste," where it does not reflect Thy glory. But our eyes are dim. We cannot see Thee as Thou art in nature. We are incapable of discerning what is Thy beauty from that which is not Thine.

"Thine is the glory." And "the Spirit searcheth all things, even the depths of God." Thy Holy Spirit is "the Spirit of glory;" and whatever is revealed to us by that Spirit, whatever is Thine, unmixed and unadulterated, that is glory, and reflects the face of Jesus Christ. But even "His visage was so marred more than any man, and His form more than the sons of men," that those who saw Him on earth saw not Thy glory. Very few have seen Him from this earth since He departed. And of those few, the one who saw most, and whom he loved the best, when he saw Him, "fell at His feet as dead."

We do "with unveiled face behold *as in a glass* the glory of the Lord;" but it is as in a mirror. We look at the mirror which reflects it. It may even make our own faces shine. But we do not yet see "face to face." "Father, I will that they also whom Thou hast given Me, be *with Me where I am, that they may behold My glory* which Thou hast given Me."

Our own share in that glory is not yet apparent. "It *doth not yet appear*"—it has never been openly displayed "what we shall be;" but we know that if it were to appear, "we shall be like Him, *for we shall see Him as He is.*"

The restoration of the Divine beauty to men as God's children is one of the great promises of the New Testament. There we learn that sin is our loss of the Divine beauty. We are sinners by so much as we "fall short of the glory of God." The attainment of our Lord as the Son of Man, in holiness, is the only perfect human example of the Divine glory. And even that was enshrined in a "body of humiliation" so long as it was manifested to the world. After He put on "the body of His glory," He was unseen except by chosen witnesses. And we have had no perfect standard of the Divine glory since His departure, except the written record of His life. How much of the Divine beauty of that record escapes our notice! How much is mis-read and misunderstood! How often we are presented with "Lives of Christ" which are but caricatures drawn by men's fancy, directing our attention to a Christ of man's invention, rather than to the true glory of the Word of God.

The Holy Spirit is the only "Spirit of glory." Only in what is revealed and taught and inspired by Him is there anything of the Divine likeness. And "we have this treasure in earthen vessels" always, while we live here. "*Thine* is the glory," and not ours. We cannot see Thy face, for "there shall no man see Thee and live." Thou hast "made all Thy goodness to pass before us," in the life of Thy Son Jesus Christ. And Thou hast proclaimed the name of the Lord before us. But none can say Lord Jesus—none can name that name intelligibly but by the Holy Ghost. We have, however, "the hope of glory." And what do we mean by this? Is it the hope of victory, or honour, or power, or authority, which we may display hereafter? Is it a white robe, a crown, a throne, or a sceptre, or the power to fly in the midst of heaven like the angels? Is it a body with a perfect organism, beyond the reach of decay, or weariness, or sickness, fitted for an eternity of enjoyment, and without any need of rest? Or is it a beautiful heavenly home, with all that is pleasant and desirable around us? Our hope includes all these things and more than all. But none of them, not even "the crown of glory that fadeth not away," *is the glory itself.* The glory that we want is the Divine likeness in our hearts and lives. "Ye shall be Holy, for I am Holy"—"perfect, as your Father in heaven is perfect." This is our first hope. Make us like Him in Spirit, and the glorified spirit will soon find a robe of glory that it may fitly wear. The Bride of Christ would look beautiful in any dress, only let her first become "a help-meet for Him," "a bride adorned for her husband" with the beauty of Holiness. Then she will be ready for the jewels and the clothing of wrought gold. The "spirit of glory" within is the only thing that will maintain the glory unsullied on the outside. But the "divine nature" will keep that glory when it has become ours. The "exceeding greatness and preciousness" of God's promises consist in the prospect of being made "partakers of the Divine Nature," when we have "escaped the corruption that is in the world through lust." Then we shall be able to see God's glory. Then, His will being done in us, and our whole nature working with it, we shall see what is in harmony with it elsewhere. Then, if He give man the dominion for which He made him—"dominion over the works of His hands"—God's will will be done on earth as it is in heaven. "The kingdom" being set up, and "the power" granted, "the glory" will soon begin to shine. Everything that comes short of His glory will be brought up to the Divine standard. He will "renew the face of the earth" after the laws of true beauty, which will then be perfectly understood. And, since beauty admits of infinite variety without disturbing its harmony, there will be endless occupation within the limits—if there are limits—of the created universe. "O *Lord* our Lord, how excellent is Thy Name in all the earth—if thou do but set Thy glory above the heavens." Exalt Him that is the Lord of glory into the place of authority; let the kingdom come, and the power, and let Him come in power and glory, and then the glory of God will overspread the face of His dominion, as the waters cover the sea.

It is only when we glorify our Father as He is, that we can truly use or appreciate what He has. His kingdom and His power both take their character from His glory. A kingdom without power is helpless. Saul when David left him was a fearful example of this. And power without authority is either lawless, or else its hands are tied. If not lawless, it is like David as a fugitive, outlawed. The kingdom and the power together may be tremendous. But what if there is no fixed character in the seat of the kingdom? Uncertainty of action combined with irresistible power may drive men to madness. But if He who has the kingdom and power has also unchanging holiness, how glorious will His kingdom be. That God should have chosen man to be His image and glory is a wonderful thing. "The dust of the earth on the throne of the Majesty on high" was a thought too great for the grasp of God's ancient people. When He descended into the dust, that He might raise us to the throne of His glory, they were offended at Him. But the gospel of our salvation is a gospel of creation as well as of redemption. The glory which belongs to our Lord from heaven, as the last Adam, was given Him before the foundation of the world. In Him God chose His people "before the foundation of the world, to be *holy* and without blame before Him in love." And all is "to the praise of His glory." When therefore we say, "Thine *is* the glory," we may well remember that from eternity He designed it for us, and gave it to us in the Person of His Son, through the working of His Holy Spirit—"the spirit of glory" that "rests upon us."

What beautiful imagery is employed in Holy Scripture to describe the coming of the Spirit of Divine glory to the dust of the earth! It is the wind blowing where it will. When man, without life, is perfect in his form and organisation, every bone and sinew in its place, and the flesh covered with the skin above—still one prayer is needed—a prayer for the Divine Spirit: "Come from the four winds, O Breath, and breathe upon these slain that they may live." Not until that prayer is answered, does the Divine image stand up on its feet, "an exceeding great army!"

The beauty of the *garden* is not complete without this breath of the Lord. "Awake, O north wind, and come, thou south; blow upon my garden, that the spices thereof may flow out."

And once more, what a beautiful emblem is that "living water" of which our Lord spoke when He promised the Holy Spirit. "The water that I shall give him shall be in him a well of water springing up (*leaping* is the very word used—leaping on) into everlasting life." There is hardly anything beautiful in natural scenery that is not associated with this description, following in the train of this word. The "living water" leaps first from the high mountain, and marks its side with a long silver streak, or it bubbles up near some resting-place on the mossy slope beneath the mountain-tops. And presently it wears a deep channel, and goes on still "leaping" down steep falls, over great stones, and round the sharp angles of precipitous crags. Leaping on still, it becomes a river, and pursues its swift and steady course, broadening into a lake, or deepening some narrow channel, flowing quietly where it is not opposed, but ready to overleap the least or the greatest obstacle. Thus the spring of living water travels to the ocean, the eternal home of all waters—"leaping on unto eternal life."

How the beauty of natural life is exhibited by this image! Yet it is but an image of the beauty that attends the growth of holiness in the soul. "Truly the glory of the Lord shall endure for ever—the Lord shall rejoice in His works." But we cannot celebrate it. We may "glorify the Lord and exalt Him as much as we can." But "even yet will He far exceed." We can "never go far enough." And therefore we will sum up all in the words of our blessed Saviour, "Thine is the glory." Father, glorify Thy Name, Thy Holy Name—"on earth as it is in heaven."

For Ever.

FOR ever in this place means "to all worlds or ages." It is hardly possible to refer to this expression in the present day without suggesting a difficulty to some minds. The words "æon" and "æonian" have been dragged from their resting-place in the Greek language, and forcibly exposed to English readers in the attempt to prove that our English Bible, when it speaks of "everlasting," "for ever," and "for ever and ever," goes beyond the truth. These familiar expressions, we are told, mean more to our ears and thoughts than the original words for which they stand. In the Revised New Testament, the word "eternal," which is properly Latin, has almost displaced the simpler English expression "everlasting." And it was evidently the Revisers' intention to suggest that, though "everlasting" means "never-ending," *eternal* may sometimes mean something less.

One simple consideration may suffice to dispel the delusion that "everlasting" is not a Scriptural idea. The idea of never-ending existence is ingrained in our nature. No civilised language can be without words to express this notion. And Greek, which is the language of the New Testament, was the language of politics and philosophy, of moral and mental science, of physics, metaphysics, history and poetry, in the ancient world. It was *the* chosen tongue of abstract thought and high civilisation. That "everlasting" should have no place in *that* language is inconceivable. No man who knows anything whatever of Greek literature could maintain such an absurdity for a single moment. It must be said that *mankind* has no notion of eternity, before it can be said that the Greeks had none. Whatever power of conceiving existence without end belongs to us, belonged quite as much or more to them. And when they had occasion to speak of that which is "everlasting and never-ending," what words did they employ? The question admits but one answer: *They used the very words which are so translated in our New Testament.* If they did not mean what they said, no more do we.

Still, it is undeniable that the *form* of the expression which is translated "for ever" is less simple than our own way of putting it, and contains some notions which are not easily grasped. The New Testament scarcely ever speaks of that which is everlasting without reminding us of *another world.* The "life everlasting" is "the life of the world to come." "He shall never die" is "he shall not die, no, not so long as the world lasts;" "the world" not being this world, but any world at all, any form of existence in which he has a portion; or, perhaps, "the world to come." And in this doxology we say, "Thine is the kingdom, the power, and the glory," *unto the worlds;* that is, "unto the end of all worlds," so long as any kind of being lasts; while anything lives at all. Sometimes the expression is even stronger, "unto worlds of worlds;" or, "unto the worlds of the worlds;" that is, unto the farthest bounds of life and being either in time or space.

The word which I am attempting to explain is in the Greek "*æon.*" It has always occasioned some perplexity; and we have no English word exactly corresponding to it. The word "world," when used in a limited sense, as I have used it in the previous paragraph, comes nearest to it. But it should be remembered that "world" has at least two other meanings, which must be kept perfectly distinct. It means the globe on which we live, and sometimes the whole sphere of being, the universe. And it also means the particular system under which we live at present, while Satan is "the prince of this world"—the "world" that "lieth in wickedness."

But the Greek for this last is "Cosmos," not Æon; and the habitable globe is the "earth." The "Universe" is not directly described by any one word in the New Testament.

Returning to the word "æon," the present "world" and the "world to come," we find that its primary meaning (as appears by its use in ordinary Greek) is the lifetime of some being or other. Every king has his "reign" as apart from his natural existence. Or, to quote a familiar proverb, "every dog has his day." The king's *reign*, and the dog's *day*, are their respective *æons.* When used absolutely, the present world or *æon* is the day of the present state of things, while Satan is prince of this world. The world (*æon*) to come is not Satan's. It belongs to another. It is His world who "shall reign over the house of Jacob for all *æons;* and of His kingdom there shall be no end."

We may go a step further, and say that a world or *æon* can have no existence of its own; because it is not itself a being, but the time or sphere in which any particular being has his way. There is no "reign" without a king, and in the proverb, a *dead* dog can have no "day." "A living dog is better than a dead lion," because the lion's day is over. The living dog's opportunities are not exhausted so long as his day lasts. In the same way, there is no such thing as "time" apart from that which keeps or makes it. If nothing moved or changed, we could not keep time. *There is no way to mark time except by motion.* Break the mainspring of the timepiece, or take away the weights, and the clock ceases to *keep time,* because it cannot go. When we ourselves are sound asleep, time for us has no existence. Or else we keep time by our dreams, a time which is altogether false, and bears no relation to the time of the outside world. A whole hour in a dream does not take a minute by the clock.

Now, the chief New Testament word for time, the word *æon,* will always remind the thoughtful reader of these things. The present world has its day, but it is passing away. "The time is *short.*" It is spoken of as dead, it is folded up for burial; it is only waiting for those who are appointed to come and carry it away. Those who belong to it, whose whole soul is wrapped up in it, will have to face another *æon* which is not theirs. Its life is the being of the last Adam, not of the first. It is His day, "the day of the Lord."

If then we can find any being whose life is beyond the reach of natural convulsions, who need not die with this present state of things, it is clear that he will have more than one *æon*. Not to-day only, but every day is His day. And first of all, this kind of Being is found in God. He is "the King of the Æons"—"which is, and which was, and which is to come." He only hath immortality, *undyingness*. And this immortality belongs to God in all the three Persons. By His Son God "made the Æons." The "days" of being are but passing hours in the lifetime of the Son of God. Whatever change of being there is in creation, He orders it. "He changeth the times and the seasons" in the history of this present world. "He removeth kings, and setteth up kings." But He Himself is "the same yesterday, and to-day, and unto all Æons," all the days of all beings that have their day under His rule. And the succeeding *Æons* do not make their successors, as kings sometimes bequeath their crowns before they die. "Through faith we understand that the *Æons* have been adjusted *by the Word of God*, so that what is seen (the visible world about us) hath not been made, or come into being, out of things that do appear." All the successive *Æons* are the production of the mind and will of their Creator. "It is He that hath made us, and not we ourselves." Neither we nor any of God's creatures are self-made or made by things below us. It is a strange belief that the lower creatures have made the greater, when the greater cannot make the less. All the men in the world could not, by their united efforts, make one monkey. And yet we are sometimes asked to believe that the efforts of the monkeys have produced the men!

"Thine is the kingdom, the power, and the glory," into the ages, or *æons*. The word "ages" might be employed to represent the Greek in this place, but for one objection. *Ages* may be mere lengths cut from the reel of time or eternity, without the idea of different states of being, distinct lives, the lives of different creatures, which the word *æon* contains. Besides, different ages are always successive. The nineteenth century and the eighteenth do not go on together. But different *æons* may run their course at the same time. Those who depart hence to be with Christ enter another world, a different *æon*, the moment that they are "delivered from the burden of the flesh." They are different beings. They live a different life. Our life is the life of this world. Theirs is the life of another. The distinction is well expressed in that saying of St Paul: "The things which are seen are temporal" (transitory); "the things which are not seen are eternal" (æonian). It may be asked, however, and this is the only part of the difficulty which is really perplexing, how the word *æonian* can mean everlasting or eternal. Literally it means belonging to an *æon*, or to *æons*. In the New Testament it seems to signify that which belongs *to one æon* no *less than to another;* that which is not destroyed by the substitution of one day for another; that which abides when king gives place to king, and world to world. In this sense only can God be called *æonian*. It is not so much because He is God in all worlds, as because all worlds belong to Him.

Whoever else may reign for a time, or "have his day," all days are but moments in the life of the Almighty. He is *æonian* in this sense only, and other persons and things are *æonian* in so far as they partake of His nature, and remain from world to world as part of the Divine plan.

From the New Testament point of view then, the "worlds" may be regarded as "dispensations," that is, *lives* which God allows to *mankind* under certain conditions. But all these "lives" are determined by successive manifestations of His Son, Jesus Christ. He is "the Father of the *æons*, or worlds." By Him "God made the *æons*." In what form He manifested Himself in "the old world" we know not; but all that is there recorded agrees with what we read of His manifestation to the patriarchs, and to Israel as the Angel of the Covenant, the Angel of Jehovah, "the Man that is the Fellow" of the Lord of Hosts. His birth as the Son of man introduced a fresh *æon*, or dispensation, in which the things of the former *æon* that had an element of the Divine life lived on, while other human accessories passed away. The time of our Lord's bodily presence on earth passed in a single "generation," as we measure time. But for its results it was equal to a thousand generations. All the ages of the former *æon* since the creation did not effect what was accomplished in the three and thirty years of the life of JESUS CHRIST. And since He glorified as the "last Adam" that form of being, we have had the dispensation of the Spirit, a third *æon*, with distinctive features, but still retaining all that was really *vital* of what had been before. We look forward to the coming of our Saviour to introduce another *æon*. And Scripture foretells yet another, when He shall have delivered up the kingdom to God.

Besides, in relation to "the god of this world," *all æons* from the creation of Adam to the second coming of Christ may be regarded as *one æon*, "this present evil world." When Satan is finally dethroned there will be a new *æon*, wherein the Lord shall be King over all the earth, and "the saints of the Most High shall take the kingdom," and possess it for ever.

It may be asked what is meant when we read in the New Testament that those who believe on the Son of God "have eternal (*æonian*) life?" Is it only that they have begun an existence which will never end? Surely it is more than this. When it is said, "this is life eternal, to know Thee, the only true God, and Jesus Christ whom Thou hast sent," we do not simply understand that those who know Him will live for ever, but that they have already in them and have begun to live here *a life which belongs to another world*. In other words, "Ye are dead" (ye died with Christ), and "*your life is hid with Christ in God*." It is hid, because men cannot see it. For all that we can see, the existence of a believer on earth is the same with that of any other child of Adam. But he has another life which we cannot see. An existence independent of "death, and sorrow, and crying, and pain," which will go on to the next *æon* and *the next*, and which is part of the life of God Himself. It is *æonian*, because no change of æon can bring it to an end.

It may be thought that this discussion has taken us far out of the lines of the Lord's Prayer. But it is not so. We cannot "pray with the understanding" unless we know what we mean. The Lord's Prayer lies both above and within our understanding. When we speak to our Heavenly Father in His own language, we are like children using words which He has taught us, calling things by the names He gives them, but not yet old enough to understand all that those names mean. "When I was a child, I spake as a child, I understood as a child, I thought as a child." It is childhood with us now. And we understand only "in part." When we see Him who taught us to pray "face to face," we shall "know even as we are known." Now we pray to a Father whom "no man hath seen at any time." Yet he that hath seen Jesus Christ "hath seen the Father." We look up to a heaven that is "within the *vail*"—a vail which we have never passed. And yet we have a hope "that entereth into that within the vail," and "boldness to enter into the Holiest by the blood of Jesus, by a new and living way." We pray that *a Name* may be hallowed which only God's Spirit can teach our hearts to lisp, and we ask for the presence of a holiness which we could not approach uncovered, "lest we die." We implore the coming of a *kingdom* which is *not of this æon*, and which is therefore outside our knowledge, for we have never lived under its sway. And we ask for the accomplishment of *a will* which is quite beyond our comprehension, and which we trace chiefly by the points at which it crosses ours.

Of *daily bread* we know something, and yet we have to live not by what we know, but by what we know not—by "every word that proceedeth out of the mouth of God." When we say, "Forgive us our trespasses," we may feel something of our sins against God, and of the sins of others against us. But we understand neither that forgiveness which blots out the memory of debt ("their sins and their iniquities will I *remember no more*") nor the extent of the debt which is forgiven. "We come short"—how far short we have no means of knowing, because we have never seen the standard—"of the glory of God." We have no perfect measure either of sin or love. When we say, "Lead us not into temptation," we refer to an invisible tempter; we ask for a leading which "brings the blind by a way that they know not;" and yet we know nothing more surely than that the sorest sting of sorrow is temptation to sin. Is "Deliver us from evil" any more within our grasp? "The origin of evil" is a very by-word and proverb for a problem that men cannot solve. The evil one's very existence is disputed. "The Deliverer" is one whom, if we love, we have not seen. Does it not become us, when we speak to Him who is invisible, of so much that we do not know, to wind up our petitions with an acknowledgment that we speak of what He knows? "For *thine is* the kingdom, and the power, and the glory, *unto all worlds.*" We have some slight glimpse of the bearing of these our supplications on the world in which we live. But Thine are all worlds, and all that is in them. The Name unchangeable, the "kingdom that cannot be moved," the will that worketh all things, are the same in every æon. Whatever comes or dies, *they are.* "For the sake of thy will," all things "that are created, *are, and were created.*" "Thine *is* the kingdom, the power, and the glory, for ever." That we should have any interest in things *eternal* is truly marvellous. It can only be, because we are "His offspring, to whom all things in heaven and earth do bow and obey." But if we may say, "Our Father which art in heaven," all the rest follows. If prayer from human lips can soar so high, is it any wonder that it should reach so far? If this God is *our* God, He must be so "*for ever and ever.*" If there is any lasting relationship between us, He must be "our Guide over death."

Amen.

—o—

THE word "Amen" is in itself exceedingly interesting. Its meaning in our English Catechism is taken from the Greek translation of the word in the earliest *version* of the Old Testament. "Let it come," or "so be it," or "let it be done." The same verb is found in the third petition, Thy will "*be done*."

But the word is originally Hebrew. It takes us back to the days of Moses. It appears first in the wilderness, where the assent of the people to the curses of the law of God was required. Many a time since the days of Joshua must the slopes of Ebal and Gerizim have resounded with the "Amen," twelve times repeated (twice twelve if we accept the Talmudical tradition that every curse had its corresponding blessing)—an Amen for each of the twelve tribes.*

Its next appearance is in connection with the establishment of the worship of God at Jerusalem with Psalms of praise (1 Chron. xvi.) Three of the books of the Psalter end with an "Amen" twice

* See Deut. xxvii. 15, &c., and a note in Bishop Ellicott's Old Testament Commentary for English readers.

repeated. The fourth ends with the combination "Amen, Hallelujah." The fifth ends with "Hallelujah" alone. The same combination appears in Revelation xix. 4. I have seen a beautiful sermon on these two words, taken as expressing man's resignation to the Divine will, and his thanksgiving for Divine mercy. They seem, as it were, to sound different notes, suitable to different times and experiences and states of mind. "Thy will be done" is "Amen." "Father, I thank Thee that Thou hast heard me" demands a Hallelujah. But again, the word "Amen" was used in a special way by our Saviour. "Amen I say unto you;" or more emphatically, "Amen, Amen, I say unto you." It is one of the few words of His native language as Jesus of Nazareth which have been preserved in the Gospel. These words are singularly precious, whether they are names given to His disciples, like Kephas, or Boanerges; or Ephphatha, with which He opened the deaf ears, and loosed the stammering tongue; or the words with which He called a child from slumber with a voice that waked the dead, while yet He spoke as gently as a mother, or a shepherd with a lamb, *Talitha Cumi*, "Wake up, little one," or "Little lamb, arise." In His sore distress also He had recourse to the cry of "*Abba* Father," and again, *Eloi, Eloi, lama sabachthani*, on the cross. The words "*Amen, Amen,* I say unto you," belong to the same list.

Note.—*Talitha*, taken as Hebrew, is a lamb, and recalls Isa. xl. 11. "He shall gather the lambs (*telâim*) with His arm." Taken as Aramaic or Chaldee, it means a "little girl," a "child."

And this word "Amen" is also a name which our Lord has taken to Himself. "These things saith *the Amen,* the faithful and true Witness, the beginning of the Creation of God." In view of this fact, who can say "that the Lord's Prayer is not offered in the Name of Jesus?" *Its closing word is His Name.*

The fact that He has thus named Himself *Amen,* shows the true meaning of the word. It takes a whole man to say "Amen." It is not merely a word, it is a description of the whole being of One that is "faithful and true." And here we may glance at its derivation. It comes from the verb *âman,* which means, in the first place, to *nurse,* or *to support.* To put the arm underneath a child to carry it, and support its weight and nurse it, is, in Hebrew, *aman.* The weight of the prayer, to which our Lord bids us lend the support of our arm, is more than we can carry. But since our Saviour has taken to Himself this Name, we may well hear Him say, when we take it upon our lips, "The Eternal God is thy refuge, and *underneath are the everlasting arms.*" Our prayers are only appeals to the promises of our heavenly Father. And whatever promises He has made, in Christ is man's only claim to them, and "in Him is the Amen," the assurance of them, "unto the glory of God by us." Thus the addition of this word "Amen" puts our hand into our Heavenly Father's, and signifies our assent to His glorious work. When we say "Amen," moreover, we bind ourselves to support our prayers by our efforts, to the full extent of the power which God gives us. We have "spoken with our mouth," we must "fulfil it with our hand" also, as far as it lies in us to be "fellow-workers with God." We bind ourselves by that Amen, *to live as we pray.*

The word Amen comes to us, not only from the Lord's Prayer, but as a familiar part of the Jewish services. "The Amen" was well known to St. Paul. And, in later times, the Rabbinical writers attached a superstitious reverence to the use of it, as appears by the following passages. "Every one who responds Amen with all his might, they open the gates of the garden of Eden to him." And again, "'The righteous nation which keepeth the truth' (Isaiah xxii.) *means* those who say the true Amen!" Strange as this way of putting the matter may seem, and superstitious as it is, it serves to remind us of the truth that the Amen uttered by our lips pledges our lives; that every one who follows the example of our Master Jesus Christ will be a living Amen to the Lord's Prayer. The Jews attached a distinct value to its use, according as it was uttered slowly or rapidly. And they had a saying, "Greater is he who responds Amen, than he who blesses (or prays)." Certainly, the mere utterance of the prayer, without the consent of the heart and life which Amen implies, is valueless.

At the same time, great as is the weight and meaning of "Amen," it will one day give place to "Hallelujah." What "Amen" is to a promise, in the language of faith and hope, that "Hallelujah" is to the fulfilment of the promise, in the language of thanksgiving. It is not only that we can say "Amen" to what God has done, when we cannot always rise to the height of "Hallelujah;" but we can say Amen to the words of promise when the time for Hallelujah is still to come.

It is very significant that the five books of the Psalter should rise gradually from Amen by itself, through Amen coupled with Hallelujah, to Hallelujah alone. Faith must give place to sight, and promises to accomplished facts, before we can see that Hallelujah is the appropriate word. And since the Lord's Prayer contains no Hallelujah, we may perhaps venture to anticipate a time when some higher strain will take its place. At least, the absence of Hallelujah may remind us once more that the Lord's Prayer was made for sinners. The absence of holiness, the presence of lawlessness and disobedience, the debt unpaid, the life divided into days by intervals of darkness, the conflict with temptation, the oppressive atmosphere of a world that "lieth in wickedness," are all suggested by the petitions of the Lord's Prayer. The doxology reminds us of a better state of things above, a place prepared for us, a kingdom and glory to which there is a possibility of access for us. But the Amen belongs less to the doxology than to the petitions which have gone before. The doxology gives a reason for the petitions. The Amen declares that we are in earnest in asking them. And when we in our services conclude the Lord's Prayer, as it is concluded in St. Luke, without a doxology, we are still accustomed to add the "Amen."

It is remarkable that when our Saviour calls Himself "the Amen," He is about to rebuke a certain church for *lukewarmness*. In two ways He assails the evil of the Laodicean church with His own goodness. He urges His own warm affection upon their indifference when He says, "As many as I *love* (dearly love) I rebuke and chasten." He rebukes their unreal profession of religious self-sufficiency with His own intense reality. "These things saith the *Amen*, the faithful and true Witness"—the *Martyr* who sealed His testimony to the truth of His confession with His blood! If this allusion is recognised, the closing word of the Lord's Prayer recalls not only the Name of Jesus, but the shedding of His precious blood. Is it accidental that the last time Amen fell from His lips in the Gospel, it was to assure the first of His apostles that he also would be faithful unto death? "*Verily, verily* (Amen, amen), I say unto thee, when thou wast young, thou girdedst thyself, and walkedst whither thou wouldest: but when thou shalt be old, thou shalt stretch forth thy hands and another shall gird thee, and carry thee whither thou wouldest not. This He spake, signifying by what death he should glorify God." And then He added, "Follow Me." These were the words introduced by the last Amen of the Gospels. They make the disciple, like the Master, "an Amen, a faithful and true Witness," "even unto prison and unto death." They remind us that once before our Lord had said to the same disciple, "Thou canst not follow Me now, but thou shalt follow Me afterwards." Then He refused His Amen to His disciple's profession of readiness to lay down his life for His sake. Now He granted it. "Amen, amen, I say unto thee," thou shalt follow Me till thy hands are stretched out for the last time to die upon the cross. "Follow me." Does not this suggest the thought that the Lord's Prayer needs to be *learnt* as well as repeated; learnt not with our lips only, but with our lives? Shall we not do well to note that Amen is not the *first* word in it, but the last? Many of our Lord's sayings *began* with "Amen." He might have taught us to begin His prayer in the same way: "*Verily, verily,* I ask Thee, O Father, that Thy name may be hallowed, Thy kingdom come, Thy will be done on earth as it is in heaven." But He who "knoweth our frame," knew that we should often need the whole prayer to strengthen us to *mean* the words that we use. Often we cannot give our whole souls to Him when we kneel down to pray. And this feeling of sinfulness—yes, of a real love for sin in our sinful hearts—is sometimes employed by the tempter to shut our mouths, and keep us from appealing to our Father in heaven. Let us remember, when thus tempted, that our "Amen" does not begin the prayer, but concludes it. "Lord, I believe, help thou mine unbelief," was answered by a miracle which amazed all the beholders with "the majesty of God." If we cannot begin with Amen, we may find grace to say it before the close. And it is no small comfort to be reminded by the very form of the prayer, that our Lord did not mean us to speak beyond our experience, or to make any professions that are untrue. If only when we say the prayer, its several petitions would rise before us in all their fulness, and we could realise what God meant us to ask for, and what He has designed to give, then we might perhaps have a mind to the Amen by the time the prayer was completed. Our heavenly Father "knoweth what things we have need of before we ask Him." And He meant to grant them too, or else why did He show His Son Jesus Christ this wonderful prayer, and bid Him teach us to pray after this manner, and to say these words? He did not ask us to put our hands to it without His. We support His cause only because He supports ours. He is not only our Father, but our *nursing-father* (our Omên, as the Hebrew has it *). And if, like our Lord's disciple, we must grow old before we can love His will as we love our own lives, yet did He not say Himself, "Even to your old age I am He, and even to hoar hairs will I carry you: I have made, and I will bear; even I will carry, and will deliver you? Thou shalt stretch forth thy hands (to support My will), and another shall gird thee, and carry thee whither thou wouldest not. Be thou faithful unto death, and I will give thee a crown of life." And in that day thou shalt no more say "Amen," without adding "Hallelujah."

* The verb *âman* in Hebrew combines the two ideas of *truth* and *belief.* From its primary meaning, "*to support*," comes the idea of solidity, firmness, reliability, and so of *truth.* Another conjugation of the same Hebrew verb means *to believe.* Just as it is said by St. John, "He that *believeth not* God, hath made Him a liar;" so, in the language of the Old Testament, He that believeth God, or trusteth God, hath made Him to be true. This is one thing which we are called to do, when we say "Amen" to the Lord's Prayer. "What things soever ye desire when ye pray, believe that ye receive them, and ye shall have them." "He is God, the faithful God" (*nĕ'ĕmân*). Let it not be said of us, "ye *believed* Him not" (ye counted Him unfaithful)! These two clauses are examples of the double meaning of the same root.

Lord, Teach us to pray, as John also taught his Disciples.

—o—

THE fragment of the history of John the Baptist which is given us in this verse ought not to be forgotten. John the Baptist is the only prophet in Scripture of whom the Bible tells us that he taught his disciples to pray. In this, as in other things, he is a great example to Christian ministers. There is no telling *what* may come of work like this—*teaching men to pray*. There is no force within man's control like the power of prayer. Men of science may argue as they will. They may not believe, and we may not be able to explain, the laws by which prayer works. But when we say that it *does work*, we know what we are saying. It is a simple fact that a few words spoken to our Lord Jesus Christ, or to our Father in heaven, have done more for him who has spoken them than all the science, and learning, and wisdom, all the rules, and methods, and remedies, that man's experience or man's invention can provide. The fact that prayer is not machinery, and cannot be taken to pieces, and explained like machinery, makes no difference to its power. It is a *power*—we know it by experience. And there the controversy ends, for every one who can pray. And when men argue against the use of prayer, or against the effect of it, they only prove that they do not know how to pray themselves. Would any sane man argue that walking is impossible if he could walk himself? That there is a *secret* in prayer is certain. But that is a very different thing from its being impossible. There is not a saint in heaven or on earth who does not know this secret. But the only two human beings in Scripture who are said to have *taught it* are John the Baptist, and our Lord Jesus Christ.

"Lord, teach us to pray." The words imply three things at least. *First*, that it is *possible* for men to pray. *Secondly*, that we cannot pray of ourselves, that we *need to be taught how*. *Thirdly*, that the Lord Jesus Christ knows how, and that *He can impart the secret to us.* I am sure I need not attempt to prove that it is possible. If we believe God's word, we know that men have prayed; and what man has done, man may do. Look at Abraham drawing near to the Judge of all the earth to plead for Sodom! Look at Jacob wrestling all night with the Angel of Jehovah, that Man who is the Lord from heaven, that he might be delivered from the hand of his brother Esau. Look at Moses, "God's chosen, standing before Him in the gap," time after time, and pleading for Israel successfully to turn away God's wrathful indignation lest He should destroy them. Look at Noah, Daniel, and Job; each of them saving lives by prayer and intercession. "The time would fail me to tell" one tenth part of all the prayers in Holy Scripture, to which the answers are recorded.

No one can believe the Bible without holding that it is possible for men to pray.

But though this is certainly possible, it is no less certain that of themselves men do not and cannot pray. They need to be *taught* to pray. And they cannot "teach every man his neighbour, and every man his brother," to do this. Most of us learnt from our mothers to kneel down and speak to Him who made us, to say the words that are meant to reach His ear whom we cannot see—to speak what would be only speaking to the air, if we did not believe in a God that is everywhere present. Thus far at least we join in the acknowledgment of the Psalmist: "O Thou that hearest prayer, unto Thee shall all flesh come." But how many of us continue to bend the knee when we arise in the morning, or before we lie down on our beds at night, and say the words that we have been taught to speak as though God were there?—how many of us continue to do this from habit, and do it for years without finding for ourselves any direct personal proof that God does hear us, or receiving in our hearts any acknowledgment of what we say? We should not be content with this kind of experience in other matters. Which of us would go on writing letters month after month, week after week—I will not say day after day—to a father or a brother whom we had never seen, who was said to be beyond the seas, and who never sent us one line of acknowledgment in return? We might hear that others had received communications from him. We might see no reason to doubt the truth of what they said. But should we really believe them? Should we go on with the apparently fruitless task? We are such creatures of habit that there is no saying what we *might* go on doing, especially if we had a sort of feeling that it would be unlucky to leave off, and that some unknown evil might befall us if we did. But would not this kind of habit be something very like a sham? If we were attacked upon the subject, should we find it easy to defend ourselves? Could we meet the onset of an unbeliever who told us boldly that there was nothing in it—that this unanswered correspondence of ours was mere waste of time and labour—that we might just as well leave it off for good and all? "Lord, *teach* us to pray." Do you begin to see what that request means, my dear fellow-correspondents with an invisible God? Do you not think it is time to inquire at head-quarters whether our letters are ever really delivered, whether they are properly addressed, whether they have been refused, or whether we may expect an answer? We do not rest content when we have posted an important communication, until we hear that it has been safely received. Ignorance upon *that* subject sometimes makes us very uneasy! Shall we rest contented with saying prayers to God whom we have not seen, every night and morning, and not make inquiries whether *those prayers are ever received* by Him, whether *they* are laid up in a store of unanswered letters, or whether He will in due time reply? There is one thing more we may be sure of. There is no such thing as a real prayer not heard before our Father which is in heaven. Our prayers do not lie in His presence like neglected letters on the table of a busy or forgetful man. One of those who learnt to pray from the Lord Jesus has said, "This is the confidence that we have in Him, that if we ask anything according to His will, *He heareth us.* And if we know that He hear us, whatsoever we ask, *we know that we have the petitions* that we desired of Him." "If we ask anything according to His will!" But then *there* is the difficulty! How am I to know what is, and what is not, "according to His will" when I pray? You need not know before you begin. Only put your hand in His, and roll your burden upon Him, and ask *everything* that occurs to you to ask. Pour out your real desires, be they what they may, as low or as lofty as you please. Only put yourselves, when you ask, entirely in His hands of whom you ask. That is what our Lord taught us in His pattern prayer. "Thy will be done on earth as it is in heaven. Give us this day our daily bread." "*Thy will* be done. *Give us*" what we need. I think I need this and this. I ask it. Give me what I ask; only not my will, but Thine be done. You would not say to Him, Not Thy will but mine be done. You cannot possibly mean that. Then ask what you will, with that proviso, and you will at least receive an acknowledgment of your letter. *You* will know that He hears you. And if you know that, you may go one step further. If your request in its present shape is not correct, He will translate it into the shape in which it ought to be. I cannot tell you how, but I can point out one or two curious instances of translated prayers in Holy Scripture. Listen to Moses when his time was come to die. It is a famous example. "O Lord God, Thou hast begun to show Thy servant Thy greatness and Thy strong hand, for what God is there in heaven or in earth that can do according to Thy works and according to Thy might? I pray Thee let me go over and see the good land that is beyond Jordan, that goodly mountain and Lebanon." That was the prayer. "I pray Thee let me go over,"—over Jordan, that is. What was the answer? NO, to all appearance. He "died there," on the same side of Jordan where he prayed, "in the land of Moab, at the mouth of the Lord." But what became of him afterwards? First there was a mysterious conflict between Satan and Michael, the archangel, over his body, and then he "appeared in glory," side by side with Elijah, who went over Jordan through the parted waters, and escaped the valley of the shadow of death. "I pray Thee, let me go over." And did he not go over? I verily believe he did. He passed out of the grave to a joyful resurrection, and before the work of God in Canaan was finished, Moses His servant was beholding His glory, not as a disembodied spirit, but with the eyes of a glorified body, in a better world. Thus God translated the prayer, which He would not answer in Moses' language, into the language of heaven, and then granted it. Elijah is another example. "He requested for himself that he might die, and said, Now, O Lord, take away my life." And did He not take it? Yes, He did after a while. He took not only the faithful soul, but the body of His servant into His glory, and anticipated the resurrection. In the New Testament there are some similar instances. "Grant that these my two sons may sit, the one on Thy right hand and the other on Thy left, in Thy glory." They "knew not what they asked." But in what striking positions they are set in Scripture history! One of them, James the son of Zebedee, was slain with the sword, first of all the twelve apostles, and departed to be with his Master. The other, the beloved disciple, remained on earth until his Master's kingdom had overspread three continents, and saw more of the spread of the gospel on earth than any of the twelve. The *first* sight of His heavenly kingdom was given to the one, the *largest view* of His earthly kingdom to the other. And thus, in a manner, they already "sit one on His right hand, the other on His left, in His glory," for heaven and earth are alike full of *that*. The prayer for the raising up of Lazarus from a bed of sickness was translated also, and answered by his resurrection, four days after burial, from the grave itself. In all these prayers the daily bread of earth was translated into the bread of heaven. But do you think any one of the persons interested, either Moses or Elijah, or James the son of Zebedee, or St. John, or their mother, or Mary of Bethany, or her sister Martha, would wish, if we could inquire of them, to have their prayers re-translated into the language in which they prayed them at first? I think not. And they are our examples, to prove that when God hears prayer, He answers it —in our own language, if that is spoken according to His word; but if not, in His language. "For my thoughts are not your thoughts, neither are your ways my ways, saith the Lord. For as the heaven is higher than the earth, so are my ways higher than your ways, and my thoughts than your thoughts."

"*Lord, teach us to pray.*" That is, we wish to know

how to pray, so that we may receive an acknowledgment that very moment, that our prayers are heard. For if we know that, we know that there is an answer coming—in our own tongue possibly, or if not, in some heavenly translation, in some version of our prayer which will make sense in heaven, and will satisfy us for ever, and ever more and more. How are we to learn this kind of prayer? Only Christ can teach us. But will He? O, yes, that He will. And how? Take a hint from St. Luke xi. 1: "As He was praying in a certain place, *when He ceased*, one of His disciples said unto Him, Lord, teach us to pray." Why do you think it is written, "When He ceased?" I cannot be sure, of course; but I know what it reminds me of. I remember that He was once "in a certain place," where He had the same wants and difficulties as ourselves while He was there. He wanted daily bread and nightly rest as we do—and work to do, and a home, and peace at home, as we do; and to be led by the right way as we do; and to be told whether He was to learn His heavenly Father's business at Jerusalem, or the business of the Carpenter at Nazareth, and be therewith content. All these wants with Him found expression in prayer. He laid them before His heavenly Father, and they were supplied. And He found peace. And greater wants than these were supplied also. Strength and patience in the anticipation of dreadful suffering, endurance through long hours of conflict, help for those whom He loved in the dark hour when they were "pressed out of measure, above strength," and hardly knew what they said or did. All these necessities came upon our Saviour "when He was in a certain place;" and He prayed, and passed safely and sinlessly through them all by the power of prayer. He never made any false prayers. "Father, I thank Thee that Thou hast heard Me, and I knew that *Thou hearest Me always*," is the record of His experience of prayer in this present evil world. And there came a time "*when He ceased*." The struggle with this world came to an end. He had no more need to send letters through the vail which severs earth from heaven, across the unmeasured space that lies between—to ask help of His Father. He overcame, and sat down with His Father on His throne. There He "liveth to make intercession for us." But we can scarcely call His intercessions in heaven and His petitions upon earth by the one common name of *prayer*. Communications between members of the same family when they dwell together in the same household, under the same roof, do not take the form of letters. That which passes between Our heavenly Father and His dear Son on the throne of God and of the Lamb in heaven is not exactly *prayer!* Even if it take the form of Divine intercession for us on the one side, and Almighty intervention on the other, it is not quite prayer. And so I say, "When He *ceased* one of His disciples said unto Him, Lord, teach us to pray." And how will He teach us? By His Holy Spirit, His representative on earth, who shall glorify Him. *He* can take of the Prayers of Christ and show them unto us. *He* can be the spirit of adoption in our hearts, whereby we cry "Abba, Father." When we know not what we should pray for as we ought, *He* can help our infirmities, and make intercession for us with groanings that cannot be uttered. And no prayer uttered, or unutterable groan which *He* inspires, can fail to receive acknowledgment. "He that searcheth the hearts knoweth what is the mind of the Spirit." Though no word is uttered, He understands, because "*He* maketh intercession for the saints *according to the will of God.*" All requests that He inspires are translated into the language of heaven, and bring down "showers of blessing" upon earth. All things touched by these prayers "work together for good to them that love God." And to pray to Him and receive acknowledgment is the way to love Him. What an experience it is! Only think of it. "In my distress I called upon the Lord, and *He heard me.*" He really did. I just spoke to Him. I had no right to do so certainly. But I told Him my case. I did not very well see what else I could do. It was desperate, disgraceful, undeserving. I need not have been surprised if He had refused to correspond with me, or even to read the communication which I sent to Him, it was so bad. But He actually heard me. He acknowledged my communication that very same day. "In *the day when I called* thou heardest me, and strengthenedst me with strength in my soul." I said, "Lord, if thou wilt, thou canst," and to my amazement He said "*I will,*" and did the very thing I asked. And now I know one thing. I know that it is possible to pray and be answered. I know the secret that Christ is able to teach—to teach us to pray. And I say to you, Try the same plan, and see if you do not succeed also. To every one of you I say, Go, and do thou likewise.

APPENDIX.

On the words for prayer in the New Testament.

[I make no apology for exhibiting Greek words in English letters, as this book is intended to reach those who are not familiar with Greek.]

The ordinary word for ***Prayer*** in the New Testament is a compound, ***pros-euché***. The verb ***to pray*** is ***pros-euchomai***. The simple word (*euché*, verb *euchomai*) seems to correspond to the English "aspiration." "I ***wish*** above all things that thou mayest prosper" (3 John 2); "I ***would*** to God that not only thou, but also all that hear me this day were such as I am" (Acts xxvi. 29);—are examples of its use. It sometimes signifies "a vow." In vows and pious aspirations we are on the border-land of prayer. These movements of the mind may become prayers at any moment. But they are not always formulated into actual prayer. And vows have been sometimes undertaken without that submission of the soul to God which is the preliminary to all real prayer.

The compound ***pros-euché***, a ***directed*** or formulated ***aspiration***, brings the soul face to face with God, and turns the eye directly to Him, instead of vaguely and indirectly to the region of things which lie outside of human control. Men may have recourse to God for many different objects. This general word "pray" or "prayer" (in Greek as in English) expresses the addressing of ourselves to Him with some direct aspiration, taking some definite shape.

The word for "worship" is different. That word (in Greek ***pros-kuneo***) describes the attitude of the worshipper towards the object of his worship. The "obeisance" or "prostration" of an Oriental before his superior is denoted by the same word. "They bow down their heads, and worship the Lord and the king" (1 Chron. xxix. 20). And *spiritual worship* is the prostration of the soul in loyal homage before "Him that ought to be feared." It may also include the deepest affection and veneration for Him who can be loved. Obviously, worship is a thing quite apart from words, or any form of words that can be devised. The Greek word for it suggests the action of the dog that fawns upon and worships his master, with abject prostration, with demonstrations of delight, or with profound devotion, according to the circumstances of the moment. And this worship may be entirely disinterested, or it may be used for a purpose. Worship, then, is the *attitude of prayer.* But worship is not actually prayer, although it is a necessary preliminary and constant accompaniment to prayer. We may notice that this word (*pros-kuneo*) is never used of Christ, except indirectly, in His answer to Satan, "Thou shalt *worship the Lord thy God*, and Him only shalt thou serve." Satan made a singular mistake, when he suggested to the Holy One to adopt an attitude towards the Prince of this world for the sake of gain, which was really lower than He was called upon to take towards His Father in heaven. Once indeed, though the word *pros-kuneo* is not used, we read that He "fell on His face" (St. Matt. xxvi. 39) "upon the earth" (St. Mark xiv. 35) when it was not enough to "kneel down" (St. Luke xxi. 41), and pray "that, if possible, the hour might pass from Him." But this was the prostration of weakness (perhaps) rather than of homage. And it was an exceptional hour even in the experience of the "Man of Sorrows."

We may take the words for prayer in the New Testament under two aspects.

First, as given by St. Paul and New Testament writers in general.

Secondly, as given by St. John.

In one well-known passage (1 Tim. ii. 1) St. Paul exhorts that "supplications, prayers, intercessions, and giving of thanks, be made for all men." There is another word for "supplications" used in Heb. v. which must be treated separately. The "supplications" of 1 Tim. ii. 1 are rather "petitions."

"*Prayers*" we have already noticed. The word is general, and is as wide in its range as the Lord's Prayer. "When ye pray (*proseuchēsthe*), say, Our Father."

Petitions ("supplications" in 1 Tim. ii. 1, Gr. *deēseis*) express the wants of the worshipper. *Worship* is what our Heavenly Father seeks for His glory. *Petitions* are what we ask for our own *need.* We cannot exactly say that the Lord's Prayer is half *worship*, half *petition.* There are petitions in the first portion. There must be worship in the last. But the *petitions* that we make in "give us," "forgive us," "lead us," "deliver us," are much more prominent than those which are contained in "Thy kingdom come," or either of the parallel clauses of the former part.

Only in connection with the night of our Lord's betrayal is the word *petition* used of Him. He "offered up *petitions* and supplications with strong crying and tears unto Him that was able to save Him from death." He said to Peter, "I *made petition* for thee that thy faith die not." Two petitions of His are visible here. One, that He might not sink under the load laid upon Him, but might be delivered from the horrible dread that overwhelmed Him; the other, that His apostles' faith might live also, and not fall to earth when they were all sifted by Satan, "sifted as the wheat." And both these petitions were granted. Let us *never forget that precedent*, when we ourselves are in utter need.

Thanksgiving (*eucharistia*) is a word that needs no explanation. Our Lord's thanksgivings, "I thank Thee, O Father," were offered both for Himself and for the babes to whom His Father had revealed Him. It was with *thanksgiving* to His Father that He spoke the invitation, "Come unto me, all ye that labour and are heavy-laden, and I will give you rest." This word "*Eucharist*" has also become a special name for "our Communion Feast."

Intercession (in Greek *enteuxis*, verb *entunchano*) is that kind of prayer in which we approach God to *interpose* on behalf of others. It is a special work of our Saviour in heaven for us, and of the Holy Spirit in our hearts. The names of "Advocate" and "Comforter," both expressed by the Greek word *Paracletos* (a legal adviser), are alike connected with this office of Intercessor. It implies some kind of equality, or at least acceptance, on the part of the Intercessor, with Him to whom he comes to intercede. In the first Old Testament example of intercession of which we have any details, we read that "Abraham *drew near* and said" (Gen. xviii. 23). The words "intercede" and "intercession" are not often used of men in the New Testament. But the duty of intercession for all men is distinctly laid down in 1 Tim. ii. 1, and our daily food "is sanctified by the Word of God and *intercession*."

Supplication (not the word in 1 Tim. ii. but in Heb. v. 7) requires special notice. It occurs only once in the New Testament, and is used in reference to our Lord's prayers in Gethsemane. Its true meaning may be seen by its associations in Greek history. The "suppliant" was a fugitive who came and sat upon the hearth of the man with whom he took refuge, and threw himself upon his mercy. This attitude was especially adopted by those who sought purification from the guilt of manslaughter. The person of the suppliant who had once taken up this position was inviolable. And the man with whom he took refuge was bound to protect him, even though he had been previously his enemy.

A *supplication* is the prayer of one who adopts this abject position. That such a word should be used of our Lord in Gethsemane is not a little remarkable. The position which he took there was ours, not His. And yet, again, it was His, not ours. For what suppliant ever had such a claim upon him to whom he had recourse, as our Lord had on Him whom he called "Abba, Father?"

In all these varieties of prayer, our Lord is our chief example. His "petitions" are also specially referred to as accompanying the supplications in Gethsemane (Heb. v. 7.)

St. John's language respecting prayer.

The foregoing words are used chiefly by St. Luke and St. Paul. Some of them are also found in other New Testament writers. But the language of St. John in reference to prayer, as also in some other important matters, brings out a fresh side of truth.

The simple word (*euchomai*), which denotes an aspiration, we have noted in 3 John 2.

The formal word for *prayer* (*pros-euchê*, *pros-euchomai*) appears only three times in St. John's writings (Rev. v. 8; viii. 3, 4), and always in the same phrase, "the prayers of the saints." That the saints do pray needs no demonstration with him. *Petition*, *supplication*, and *intercession* are all absent from his writings. But the attitude of "*worship*" is more frequently alluded to by St. John than by any other writer of the New Testament. To him we owe the description of "the true *worshippers*," who *worship* the Father in Spirit and in truth, and that most attractive saying, that "the Father *seeketh* such to worship Him." That Almighty God should so far humble Himself to behold the things that are in heaven and earth as to *seek* this affectionate adoration from men, is a truth to be pondered deeply. It is a thing to be desired with Him that we should love Him. Consider in this light the many passages where He presents Himself as "making a marriage for His Son," and not only calling men as guests to the wedding, but of them making for His Son a chosen Bride, "I will make him an help meet for him." Consider how "Christ loved the Church, and gave Himself for it, that He might sanctify and cleanse it," and in the end "present it to Himself a glorious Church, not having spot, or wrinkle, or any such thing, but that it should be holy and without blemish." Is any language that devotion has ever been able to inspire, too high for those who have been made the objects of this search for worshippers—those whom the Father has sought and found, and taught to worship Him? And is it any wonder that the word for "worship" should be of somewhat frequent occurrence in the writings of St. John? The book of Revelation in particular contains this word more times than any other book in the New Testament. In heaven, where God is seen, *He is worshipped.*

One simple word is employed by St. John for prayer on earth. "To ask" (*aiteo*) "requests or petitions" (*aitemata*) is a lesson he gives us both from himself and from the lips of our Lord. He it is who preserves the command to "ask in the name of Jesus," and the promise that whatsoever we shall ask in His name He will do, with the confidence that this gives to our prayers. St. John also uses another word for "asking" (*erotao*), which properly means to "ask questions," but also signifies "to make request" as from an equal. The mere mention of a difficulty, or a want, in certain relations, is understood to be a request, and receives immediate attention. To *ask petitions* (*aiteo, aitema*) is the beggar's task. To make requests (*erotao*) to God for us is a work which Christ has undertaken. "*I pray for them*" (literally "concerning them I ask"); "I *pray* not for the world, but for them whom Thou hast given me, for they are Thine," is an example of this use. But, in the language of the New Testament, Christ does not *worship* or *beg*. He "intercedes;" He also inquires, or He makes request (St. John xiv. 16; xvi. 26; xvii. 9, 15, 20). In the last clause of 1 John v. 16, it is an interesting question whether we should interpret the word *erotao* to mean "inquire," or "pray."

The Old Testament words for prayer, although they embrace many of the ideas illustrated above, are not so sharply or easily distinguishable in reference to their usage. Our space will not permit us to treat them adequately here.

L'Envoi.

AVDI · ANIMA · MEA ·

("Hark, my soul, it is the Lord.")

VOX · DIVINA · PVLSAT · AVREM
AVDIN' · HOMO · SALVATOREM ·
TIBI · JESVS · IPSE · FATVR ·
DILIGISNE · ME · PECCATOR ·

* VINCLIS · EGO · LIBERAVI
† SAVCIVMQVE · TE · SANAVI ·
EX · ERRORE · REDIGEBAM ·
LVCEM · TENEBRIS · REDDEBAM

NVM · QVEM · PARTVM · PEPERERE ·
DISCENT · MATRES · NON · FOVERE ·
NOSTIN' · ILLAS · OBLIVISCI ·
NOVIT · JESVS · REMINISCI ·

OMNI · TIBI · FIDVS · HORA
AMOR · CŒLIS · ALTIORA ·
MORTIS · INFIMOS · RECESSVS ·
TRANSIT · VICTOR · INDEFESSVS ·

MECVM · GRATIA · PERFECTA ·
TV · TRIVMPHOS · MOX · EXSPECTA ·
MECVM · REGE · REX · REGNABIS ·
ME · PECCATOR · NONNE · AMABIS ·

NIL · ME · JESV · TANTVM · PIGET ·
LANGVET · ARDOR · AMOR · FRIGET ·
AMO · VENEROR · MAJORE ·
AMOR · ARDEAT · AMORE ·

* Volunt alii VINCTVS. † Volunt alii SAVCIVSQVE.

JOHN F. SHAW & CO.'S

Religious and General Publications.

By Dr. H. SINCLAIR PATERSON.

"In Defence." THE EARLIER SCRIPTURES.

Crown 8vo, 5/-, cloth extra.

"No work on the Pentateuch has ever given us so much satisfaction."
Young Men's Christian Association Notes.

"The book is characterized by a simple directness, combined with a frank and fearless expression of opinion and a deep insight into the inner meaning of Scripture which should make it at once popular and in the highest sense useful."
The Christian.

"A most valuable contribution to Biblical literature, written in plain, forcible language and in the spirit of childlike faith. We trust it may be widely circulated, especially among young men."—*Woman's Work.*

"It is to be wished that this book may have a wide circulation as an able and well-written defence of the earlier Scriptures, boldly conceived, carefully elaborated, thoughtfully compressed, and considerately adapted to the general reader."
PRINCIPAL CAVE, in *The British and Foreign Evangelical Review.*

"In Defence." THE FOURFOLD LIFE.

Crown 8vo, cloth extra, 5/- Shortly.

This volume deals with the gospel narratives in the same clear and helpful manner in which the Author treated "The Earlier Scriptures."

Christ and Criticism;

OR, THE WITNESSES EXAMINED AND CROSS-EXAMINED.

8vo. Price One Shilling.

"These Lectures certainly form one of the ablest of all the contributions to the literature of the evidences that have been made in recent years. A better book to place in the hands of a thoughtful sceptic it would be hard to name."
Christian Leader.

The Highway of Holiness.

HELPS TO THE SPIRITUAL LIFE. By Rev. W. HAY M. H. AITKEN, M.A.

Crown 8vo, cloth extra, 3/-

This volume stands almost alone among this Author's well-known series as *exclusively* presenting subjects bearing on the Christian life and character.

Clear Shining Light.

Memorials of CAROLINE W. LEAKEY, Author of "God's Tenth," &c.
Edited by her Sister. New Edition. Small 8vo, cloth extra, 3/6.

"A touchingly written record of a bright and useful though often suffering life. Will be read with delight and profit."—*Church Missionary Gleaner.*

CHOICE PRESENTATION VOLUME.

Uniform with the Parchment Library.

Between-Times. Thoughts for Spare Moments.

BY LADY HOPE. Demy 16mo, 1/-

This unique little volume cannot fail to prove a welcome companion to every earnest Christian who makes its acquaintance. As a Christmas, New Year, or Birthday present, it will be most acceptable.

JOHN F. SHAW & CO., 48, PATERNOSTER ROW, E.C.

A 2

Books for Ministers and Teachers.

Ninth Edition, complete in one volume, pp. 1,040, Cloth, 9/-.

Studies for the Pulpit. Containing over Three Hundred Sermons and Outlines, with Biblical Illustrations, Counsels for Preachers, &c.

"An exceedingly valuable work."—*Rock.*

Crown 8vo, cloth extra, 3/-

Living Water for Little Pitchers.

By Rev. JAMES STEPHENS.

"Admirably suited to the purpose for which they are intended; short and animated, full of anecdote, and nearly certain not only to retain the attention, but to appeal to the affections of little hearers."—*The Guardian.*

Crown 8vo, Cloth, 3/6.

Typical Foreshadowings in Genesis.

By W. LINCOLN, Author of "Lectures on Revelation," &c.

"We trust the work will lead to much thoughtful and prayerful study." *Word and Work.*

New Edition. Crown 8vo, Cloth, 3/6.

The Satan of Scripture.

By Rev. J. ORMISTON, M.A.

"The only exhaustive work that we know of on this solemn subject." *Christian Age.*

New and much Enlarged Edition, Cloth, 7/6.

A "Living Epistle;"

Or, Letters of C. S. BLACKWELL.

"We have found much profit in reading these fragments so far as we have gone, and are promising ourselves a great treat in looking over the rest." Rev. C. H. SPURGEON.

New Edition, price 2/6, Cloth.

The Two Paths: Being a Brief Examination of Canon FARRAR's Doctrine of "Eternal Hope." By Rev. JOHN BENNETT, M.A., Park Chapel, Chelsea.

"A useful book to put into the hands of persons who have been perplexed or shaken by Canon Farrar's teachings."—*Record.*

Small 8vo, Cloth, 3/6.

Scripture Object Lessons and Outline Teaching for Sunday-schools.

By Rev. H. C. McCOOK.

"We earnestly urge every teacher to read this book, and make use of it. It is invaluable."—*The Sword and the Trowel.*

JOHN F. SHAW & CO., 48, PATERNOSTER ROW. E.C.

CPSIA information can be obtained
at www.ICGtesting.com
Printed in the USA
BVHW041336130720
583597BV00003B/179

9 781376 32650